Praise for *Make Them Smile*

"From humble beginnings in a faraway land to the pinnacle of success in America as a CEO and visionary leader, Dr. Ahmed takes readers on a moving journey through the major obstacles he faced, the challenges he overcame, and the successes he has achieved. I was captivated by his remarkable story and learned invaluable lessons on the power of leadership, optimism, and the unrelenting pursuit of excellence."

—Todd Hirsch, Senior Managing Director of
Tactical Opportunities, Blackstone

"The American Dream lives! And it lives in the spirit of Sulman Ahmed, who, as an immigrant, has done what millions of immigrants before him have done: indelibly altered the face of American society. Determination, adaptability, persistence against the worst of odds—Dr. Ahmed has it all in spades, and his story, compellingly told in this book, serves as a powerful reminder of the transformative power of diversity and the immeasurable contributions that immigrants bring to the fabric of society. I am honored to call Sulman a friend, and I deeply admire his ability to embrace the unknown and create his own opportunities and success."

—Wan Kim, CEO and Chairman of the Board, Smoothie King

"Effective leadership sits at the heart of any high-performing service business. As a leader, Sulman has no peers. I had the privilege of working with him as DECA Dental's first finance partner and discovered that, like other great leaders, Sulman contains countless paradoxes. He can command a room while relating to everyone from the biggest boardroom personalities to the humblest frontline workers. He competes, fiercely, but without alienating his allies or opponents. He manifests his future through a steadfast commitment to his vision but retains the flexibility to adapt when necessary. He's an incredible judge of character without coming across as judgmental or condescending. He's serious about life, work, and his goals but never takes himself too seriously. He can laugh about himself and his mistakes but never does so at the expense of others. He can unite people and organize them to achieve the unimaginable. His book offers us powerful lessons on how to live and lead a little more like him. I hope we're ready to listen, too, because if we do, the world will benefit."

—J. R. Davis, Managing Partner, Blue Sea Capital

"At Tufts University School of Dental Medicine (TUSDM), we aim to be global leaders in oral health and train the world's dentists. As the Dean of TUSDM, I can't think of anyone who better embodies our mission than Dr. Ahmed. He is a natural-born leader who sets an example of respect, drive, and empathy. It is this last quality that makes me most proud to be associated with him. We all should strive to embrace this human quality, and it is this quality that has driven Dr. Ahmed to be an entrepreneur and innovator. He has expanded access to top-tier oral health care throughout America and proved a shining example to dentists everywhere. And now, with this book, he has done the same for our new business leaders."

—Nadeem Karimbux, DMD, MMSc, Dean,
Tufts University School of Dental Medicine

"Sulman has done the unthinkable: scaled a medical services company without sacrificing quality of care. He knows people, he knows business, and he knows how to lead. Thanks to his vehement commitment, he has succeeded (and will continue to) in whatever he sets his mind to. Read this book. It contains knowledge that will forever help you in business and in life."

—Jay Adair, Co-CEO, Copart

MAKE THEM SMILE

MAKE THEM SMILE

Why Customer Satisfaction Is the Key to Rapid and Sustainable Growth

SULMAN AHMED

Matt Holt Books
An Imprint of BenBella Books, Inc.
Dallas, TX

Matt Holt is an imprint of BenBella Books, Inc.
10440 N. Central Expressway
Suite 800
Dallas, TX 75231
benbellabooks.com
Send feedback to feedback@benbellabooks.com

Printed in the United States of America
10 9 8 7 6 5 4 3 2 1

Library of Congress Control Number: 2023949464
ISBN 9781637745793 (hardcover)
ISBN 9781637745809 (electronic)

Copyediting by Ruth Strother
Proofreading by Rebecca Maines and Jenny Bridges
Text design and composition by PerfecType, Nashville, TN
Cover design by Brigid Pearson
Printed by Lake Book Manufacturing

Dedicated to Dr. Julie Covino Ahmed—my wife, confidant, and best friend, for always believing in me and supporting me in seeing how unbelievably fulfilling a life spent serving others could be.

And to Daniel, Sofia, Eleanor, and Rian for showing me what "right" looks like and always loving me for who I am. This book is a testament to all of you.

In honor of my parents: Riaz and Qaiser Ahmed—you instilled in me the confidence to go after my dreams and always provided a safe place called home to return to.

CONTENTS

FOREWORD

America is an amazing country in many ways, but what stands out is the level of entrepreneurship in the nation. Today there are 31 million entrepreneurs in the United States according to the Global Entrepreneurship Monitor, and that is about 16 percent of the adult workforce. Moreover, 5 percent of adults have started a business at some point in their lives. Many are successful, but many of these businesses fail.

The book you are about to read is a true story about entrepreneurship, but it is also about reinventing an industry of "necessity" to meet the needs of the customer—or, in this case, the patient. Sulman not only takes you on his personal journey from Zimbabwe to Dallas, Texas, but he also demonstrates with great examples the different strategies that need to be applied to businesses that operate at different stages of development. He takes you from start-up to midstage and midstage to maturity. In truth, you never get to maturity because the great entrepreneur continues to challenge the status quo and find ways to make their business even better.

This is not just a business textbook. Sulman tells a story about tackling an industry that needed redefining. He is focused on making DECA

Dental the "Starbucks of the dental world." He describes how he has overcome many frustrations and barriers. Sulman is truly a game changer who has succeeded. Take this book and imagine your own potential journey as you dream about becoming a successful entrepreneur.

Nigel Travis, former CEO/Chair, Dunkin' Brands

INTRODUCTION

In my elementary school, lunchtime brought about pure chaos. Every day at the bell, the students burst out of the classrooms, over the teachers' protests, and scrambled to be first in line at the cafeteria. For us, the stakes couldn't be higher. If you didn't get in line early enough to snag a chicken pie, you wouldn't eat. It might sound strange to an American audience, but that's what it was like growing up in Harare, Zimbabwe (then known as Rhodesia). My parents were doctors and able to provide me a comfortable childhood. But that didn't stop me from sitting through afternoon classes with a gurgling stomach. Or from studying by candlelight during rolling blackouts. Or biking tens of miles to compete in squash tournaments. In those days, we had to scramble to live the lives we wanted, and I've been hustling ever since.

I moved to the United States for college when I was nineteen to pursue undergraduate education. I went straight from my undergraduate commencement ceremony to my dental school convocation within two days. At twenty-five, I left dental school, failed to buy my own dental office, and ended up living in my parents' Dallas guest room. But I kept working; I kept pushing. In 2008, I officially launched my brand, Ideal Dental. By 2021, I closed a financing deal that valued my company at more than $500 million at about 85 locations.

But when I was a twenty-two-year-old dental student at Tufts, I had looked out at a very different future. Many professionals—doctors, lawyers, dentists, physical therapists, consultants—inadvertently resign themselves to lives of relentless grinding. They seek training that lands them in debt. To pay that off, they toil for years. They can only earn when they work. Worse, they can only leverage their expertise to serve clients when they work. Many dream of a different reality, one where they earn passive income and build a company that shares their expertise with more people than they ever could alone. But these kinds of service industries are by nature almost impossible to scale. Unlike manufacturing or tech, where you can create a product and then roll it out across the world, these professionals work in highly specialized service trades. They each have their own approach, and the quality of their work depends on their talent.

Seated with fellow matriculants, I realized that this most likely was the destiny awaiting all of us. I was terrified.

I knew that I wanted to build real wealth and help as many people as possible. So I resolved not to drift into the slog of private practice and to start my own brand. We've grown exponentially since we launched, and every day we serve thousands of people. We keep them out of pain and keep the wattage on their smiles dialed to max. In the first part of this book, I share how I found ways to innovate within an ancient, staid industry by putting the customer before all else. In the second part, I share reflections on how I standardized a notoriously mercurial business, and give suggestions for how you can do the same.

To the hardworking and the dedicated, this book offers a way out. A way out of the grind of working as an expert, of living billable hour to billable hour. It offers a road map for how to revolutionize an industry and standardize a process that seemed impossible to standardize.

I recommend you use this book as a framework for reflection and as a guide. Read it from cover to cover first when you're just starting out to get a sense of the journey that awaits you and what it will take for you to achieve your dreams. I'm hopeful that you'll use my story as a mirror that will help you see yourself in a new light and zero in on exactly what makes your vision unique. Then in the darkest moments, the moments when you feel alone and helpless (they, sadly, come for almost all of us), return to this book. Use it for comfort and to regain the perspective that things will improve. Read the sections that pertain to whatever stage you're in and the stage of growth you want to reach. Mine the text for nuggets of wisdom, pause frequently to consider your own situation, and discover new perspectives and approaches.

Finally, return to this book in times of triumph. Let it buoy you and remind you that whenever we reach a peak we never thought we could reach, we can stop and savor the view before we soldier on to higher and higher heights.

CHAPTER ONE

Have a Grand Vision

Discipline. Sacrifice. Intelligence. Grit. Work ethic. Creativity. Luck. These are the attributes that most people associate with success. And they're all important. But a person can display all these traits and still not reach the highest levels of achievement. That's because this list omits the most important ingredient: a grand vision—an idea of a beautiful future to strive toward. The immense promise of a grand vision accentuates every other ingredient of success. It gives shape to creativity and focuses new ideas and innovations toward a common goal. It lends meaning to the discipline and sacrifice and it is the fire that fuels the fourteen-hour workdays needed to create your own luck.

Every great business starts with the founder's grand vision. The most famous example might be Apple, which was powered by Steve Jobs's belief that computers would revolutionize how people think, communicate, and work. Your grand vision is so integral to your success that I've put it here first. There's no point getting into the steps if you don't know what success looks like to you.

My grand vision was to create the Starbucks of dentistry: a scalable, standardized retail healthcare brand. A national brand that provides such repeatable results that going to the dentist feels almost as comfortable as grabbing a venti Pike Place roast.

This was a tall task that lent grandiosity to my vision. After all, it's become a tired trope that people *dread* dentist visits. As much as this irks us in the field, it's not hard to see where it comes from. We poke needles into gums. We drill into teeth. We excavate diseased nerves. We pull out teeth. No matter how much we all work to keep our patients calm and happy, there will always be a certain level of fear involved in a dentist visit.

A lot of people go to the dentist feeling confused and vulnerable, and this is compounded when they are subjected to pain that might seem needless and arbitrary. I wanted my practice to be completely dedicated to satisfying customer needs. To create a dental office so inviting, people felt almost as comfortable as they do in their own homes. It would be standardized so that every location looked the same, smelled the same, and people would never hear a drill. A practice where people trust their dentists completely because we always deliver the best work (backed by money-back guarantees) with the greatest possible convenience.

Regardless of what your grand vision is, you can expect certain experiences that will challenge you along the way. Here are a few common ones that most successful entrepreneurs (including me) have encountered and some suggestions as to how to deal with them.

YOU WON'T FIT IN WITH THE CROWD

On my first day at the Tufts School of Dental Medicine in Boston, the dean asked the entire 150-student class, "After becoming a dentist, who wants to be an oral surgeon?" A bunch of hands went up. "Who wants to be an orthodontist?" A bunch of hands went up. "Who wants to be a pediatric dentist?" He kept listing specialties, and hands kept going up. As this went on, my first thought was, *Oh my God. How do these people even know what they want to do four years from now? I'm just glad I barely got in here.*

Two days before that meeting, I had graduated from the University of Texas at Dallas. I hadn't yet processed the fact that I was starting dental school. I could hardly imagine getting through the next several years, much less what type of dentist I wanted to be. This was when I realized that I didn't fit in with the crowd. I tried to picture myself as an oral surgeon or a pediatric dentist or an orthodontist or even just having a standard dentistry practice, but each time I drew a blank. I couldn't see myself in any of those professions.

Instead, as I watched my classmates' hands rise and fall, an idea slowly dawned on me. I was surrounded by all these talented, smart people who knew exactly what they wanted. I thought, *Wouldn't it be cool if I could have all these specialists working together with me?*

This thought became the seed of my grand vision. Even though I didn't know much about dentistry at that time, I knew it was unusual for several different specialties to share the same office. I realized I could create a dental brand that offered all services under one roof. A one-stop shop for dentistry—a completely new concept in the very early 2000s.

In all likelihood that thought arrived as a defense mechanism. I'd felt intimidated. I was surrounded by students, most of whom had been born in the US with a deep sense of certainty about the trajectory of their lives. I, on the other hand, had no idea where I wanted to go. In many ways I envied my fellow students. But as I reflect on the experience now, I realize that what I took as insecurity and envy was actually an indicator of my entrepreneurial ambition. I couldn't imagine the lives my classmates wanted because I wanted to avoid the day-to-day monotony of the life of dentistry. I wanted to impact as many lives as I could beyond just the one patient per hour I would see in my chair. In the end, I'm deeply thankful that I listened to the resistance I felt toward choosing a specialty and let myself imagine a different future.

My sense of being separate from the crowd continued after orientation. As classes started, my peers became more confident in their choices. They plodded along the usual course and started to prepare for their specialties. My few peers who, like me, had arrived at Tufts undecided quickly chose and settled on a path. I, on the other hand, fell more and more in love with the idea that I would one day build the Starbucks of dentistry. Yet whenever I brought up that plan to classmates or professors, their responses were almost universally discouraging. Some of them openly laughed; most of them raised their eyebrows and said something like, "That sounds really cool," as they moved on to other matters.

My grand vision also led me to behave differently as a student, which further prevented me from fitting in. Dental school usually takes four years, with the first two being didactic classroom teaching, and the second two being comprised of clinical practice because students must successfully complete each procedure a certain number of times. I figured I could finish in less than two years. Instead of taking term breaks, I went to the clinic to rack up more procedures. I showed up earlier than my classmates and worked later. I focused on becoming as efficient as possible. The school gave us three hours to examine, diagnose, and treat each patient. I managed to do it all in an hour and a half without any dip in my work quality, which allowed me to finish more procedures per day. I finished the two-year clinical portion in fourteen months.

I couldn't graduate early, but this offered me an important opportunity. I spent the last several months of my time as a student teacher, training third-years on basic dental techniques. In my experience, the best way to truly master a skill is to teach it. Teaching requires you to think about how to explain concepts and procedures to someone, which often forces you to think about them from angles you had never considered before. This experience made me a much better dentist and a better leader and mentor. It helped me develop the skills to train the first dentists I would hire and to get them to maintain our clinical excellence. It also showed me that I have a passion for teaching, for giving back to others, and that I could scale my impact by helping people develop confidence in their own skills to serve patients around the world.

Once I started to pursue my vision in earnest, my sense of isolation only deepened. People openly mocked me for thinking that I could create the Starbucks of dentistry. I had dental equipment vendors and banks laugh at me when I shared my vision, and they told me I'd be lucky to get to five or six locations. I never worked with those people again. The funny thing was that when my idea started to grow explosively, they all came back, they all wanted my business. But it was too late. I'd already created my own crowd, and they were all I needed.

Create Your Own Crowd

The early years of my business were marked by considerable fear, uncertainty, and failure. I often wondered if my grand vision was even possible. At the start of a journey, the gap between where you want to be and where you currently are can seem insurmountable. The more you focus on that gap, and all the traps and potential setbacks that lurk in that void, the more despondent you will feel.

We all to a certain extent doubt ourselves, especially when embarking on something new. Humans are social creatures, and you may find it invaluable to recruit a couple of people that you trust, whom you can turn to for support, and who will throw themselves with vigor into growing the business alongside you. For me in those early days, I leaned heavily on my loved ones. My girlfriend at the time, Julie Covino, who is now my wife, supported me every day. I would spend hours talking to her about my dreams, about my frustration at how long it was taking. When I had doubts, I went to her, and her faith and trust gave me the strength to continue. It was much the same with my mother and father, who I visited often to talk about my business and my experience as a dentist.

Then, professionally, I encountered several people early in my career who had faith in me and my vision and were willing to dedicate their lives to helping me build something incredible. I worked intimately with them during the start-up stage of Ideal Dental, and they contributed tremendous energy, talent, and creativity. We learned how we each think, react, and plan. They understood, almost as well as I did, the sort of culture and processes that I wanted to define our company and helped implement them in all our new offices.

The first person I partnered with was Dr. Rodney Alles, a dentist in the same office I worked in after dental school. We became friends, and I admired his dental skills. When I told him that I planned to leave, he asked what I was going to do. I explained I wanted to start the Starbucks of dentistry and watched him light up. He told me that he was tired of working in the office too, and asked if he could partner with me in an office. I agreed, and we opened an office together.

The second person was Dr. Shalin Patel, a dentist at the first office I bought. When I made the acquisition, my start-up was still not producing enough revenue, and I had initially planned on working out of the office myself so I could cover my personal debt and pay my bills. To do that, I planned on letting Dr. Patel go, so I invited him out to dinner.

We got to the restaurant and started talking. Before I could tell him I wouldn't need his services, we'd hit it off. Eventually, he asked me about my business, and I told him that I planned on building the Starbucks of dentistry. The enthusiasm of his reaction floored me. He thought it was an excellent idea and instantly started asking if he could be involved and what he could do to help me.

I could tell that his excitement was genuine. He gave off this earnest, electric energy. I knew it would be great to have him on board for the long haul because I needed people who would be willing to run through all the walls I was planning on running through. So, I kept him on. We worked together in the office, which meant I had to give up a lot of short-term income. But it was worth it.

There was something deeply sustaining about these relationships from the beginning. Now, both these doctors hold equity in DECA Dental (the holding company of Ideal Dental), and together they run the clinical side of our operations. In the early days, they helped me recruit, retain, and train elite dentists to make sure we provided the best possible care. Now they do the same, developing processes to keep our clinical work top-notch and seeking out innovations that will allow us to better serve our guests.

At this time, I also met several other clinical and business leaders who are still with the company fifteen years later. People like Cassie Jenkins, who started as a front office staff member at my first office; Carol Canava; Ester Strickland; and many others. They instantly bought into my grand vision for Ideal Dental. They rapidly became some of the best people working for us, and I relied on them to develop the culture and environment that we present to our guests, and to make sure that new hires understood how to maintain it. They played an integral role in developing the systems that allow us to serve customers with unparalleled efficiency, and the training systems that have made our entire staff notable for their kindness, patience, and care. They are now one of the major pillars of our company. Several other administrators and front office staff joined us at this time and played major roles in our growth and continue to take us forward.

There's a common saying: don't go into business with friends. In many ways, this is sound advice. But I've found that in working closely with some exceptionally talented people for years, we have naturally become close friends. They're some of the most important relationships I have, and I will cherish them my entire life.

TAKE RISKS OTHERS WON'T AND DO THINGS THAT MAKE YOU UNCOMFORTABLE

I've always believed that leaders do what other people cannot or will not do. And early in my career, I lived this maxim to the max. I took a staggering number of risks. Today, I can hardly believe that life worked out as it did. My obsession with my grand vision blinded me to the precarity of my situation, something I've discovered is true for most entrepreneurs. I was also, frankly, too young and naïve to know any better. That, and I'd left school with towering confidence after having finished the two-year clinical portion of dental school in fourteen months.

I've always believed that leaders do what other people cannot or will not do.

The one thing bigger than my confidence was my debt. Before I even graduated, I'd bought a condo in a new building in Dallas for $530,000. I had no income, but I got a loan with no money down because the lender expected I would find a high-paying job as a dentist. And because it was 2005, the peak of reckless lending by banks that would bring about the 2007 financial crisis. They were giving loans to anybody who could blink back then, no proof of income necessary. When I added my $530,000 mortgage to my $500,000 student loan debt from college and dental school, I carried over $1 million in debt before I'd even left school or got a job. But I wasn't even a little bit concerned. I was too naïve and excited to realize how precarious a situation I was in.

All that debt with no income wasn't even the biggest risk I took. In 2008, about three years after I graduated, I had managed to save about $70,000 while working as a dental associate. At that point I decided to launch my own brand. After a lot of back and forth, I landed on the name, and I designed our first logo and chose our colors. I knew I wanted to build an office from scratch, a process that took about a year and cost $800,000.

While that office was being built, I would have zero income, so I decided to buy a second office at the same time. That office cost $1.3 million. Again, I didn't have money for a down payment, so that entire amount went straight to my debt burden, which ballooned to $3.1 million.

Shortly after that, the wife of one of my friends, herself a dentist, was facing bankruptcy. She reached out to us. It was 2010, and the economy was deep into the recession. She asked if I would be interested in buying out her business. It would only cost me the money left on the note—about $250,000. This was relatively cheap, and the practice was in a great area of Dallas—an upper-middle-class neighborhood with plenty of demographic growth and young families in need of dentists. Even though my first two locations were barely profitable, I agreed to buy the office if the bank would approve the loan. The funding came through, so I bought the office. That brought my final tally to three offices and $3.35 million in debt, and I'd barely turned thirty.

But it didn't matter. I was on my way to building the Starbucks of dentistry—all of my offices were branded, they all had the same color scheme and décor, the staff wore the same-color scrubs. We provided exceptional standardized dentistry. We took utmost care of our guests. In many ways, we were successful. But I was too young and dumb to recognize I was setting myself up to fail. And fail I did.

YOU WILL FAIL. A LOT.

In pursuing a grand vision, you will, inevitably, fail. In fact, to succeed you almost need to seek out failure. By that I don't mean you should try to fail. I mean that, fundamentally, no matter what you do, when you seek success, you will cultivate failure. People who experience the fewest failures usually hold one stable job their whole life. If that were your idea of success, I doubt you'd be reading this book. So know this: what determines whether you will succeed isn't if you fail, but how you respond to the failures you'll inevitably face. In my experience, there are two keys to effectively responding to failure: don't give up, and learn from your failures.

Don't Give Up

Always keep challenges and failures in perspective. In most cases, what we perceive as a failure is in fact a temporary setback and is more often than not an opportunity to learn and grow. The only terminal failure comes when you let setbacks overwhelm you to the point that you abandon your grand vision. My career path was anything but linear. Nobody's is. But I remained focused on my primary goal even when I had to take detours. In fact, as it often happens, one of those detours proved to be one of the most important and useful experiences in my career.

I planned to waste no time and to launch my business immediately after dental school. Before I graduated, I got in touch with some brokers, and we looked for dental offices in Dallas. We found a great practice in a beautiful suburb of Dallas. It cost $1.2 million. Again, I didn't have income or collateral. Still, I applied for a loan to buy the office and was approved. As we neared our closing date, I went to the office a couple of times just to make sure that everything looked OK. On each of those visits, I heard the receptionist tell clients as they checked out, "Dr. Roberts will see you at his new office."

I got nervous. I was planning on taking out a loan for over a million dollars to buy this place and, therefore, the client list, but apparently there was a new office. I asked the outgoing dentist about it, and he said, "Well, technically I don't have to disclose this, but yes, I'm building an office about a mile and a half away, and some of the patients will come with me."

A mile and half away would put him in direct competition with me! I pulled out of the deal.

Shortly after, I graduated and moved to Dallas. My condo wasn't ready, so I moved in with my parents for a few months and got a job in a local dental office as a dental associate. In a sense, this was a failure. My life hadn't turned out as I planned. Instead of living in a nice new condo and working for myself, I lived in my parents' guest room, working for someone else. It felt like I was back in high school, only this time I had a lot more debt and responsibilities. Worse, I had spent the last several months bragging to my friends and peers about my big moves. And now I was explaining over and over why it wasn't happening. But—and this might be the most important lesson of this book—what felt like a total failure was in fact a blessing. To extrapolate, the lesson is that a truly terminal failure has little to do with external circumstances and everything to do with how you respond. A failure is merely a result that does not meet expectations. In the face of that result, you can either wilt, or you can keep the faith, stay the course, and learn whatever lessons you need to learn to achieve your ultimate goal. In this case, if I had let this failure stop me, I would have never built my company.

Reflecting on it now, I realize that if I had bought that first dental office, I most likely would never have achieved what I have. At the time, I was twenty-five and fresh out of school. I didn't know nearly enough about dentistry or business to succeed. I had honed my skills at Tufts, but I only knew how to do some of the most basic procedures. I'd say that I mastered only half of the treatments I would need to run my own office. On top of that, I didn't know how to do real-world dentistry. In dental school, we usually had professors checking our work and our diagnostics. And everything on the business side—scheduling, advertising, billing, and insurance—was handled for us.

If I had bought that location, I would have had to juggle learning more dentistry while learning how to run a business and trying to keep everything going well enough to avoid defaulting on any of my $2.2 million debt. I'd most likely still be working out of that one office today, doing everything I could to get out of my student loans. Instead, I spent two-and-a-half years as a dental associate, during which time I learned everything I could about dentistry and managed to save $70,000 in my personal checking account.

This associateship allowed me to master my craft, which gave me the knowledge I needed to build an excellent company. To be clear, there was nothing particularly unique about what I learned. It was just dentistry. But I learned to execute at an extremely high level. I refined my social and emotional intelligence, and I practiced empathy toward my patients and learned how to communicate with them. When I explained why I recommended a procedure, they almost always agreed to it right away. I helped people with their pain, helped them feel more confident in their smiles, and ultimately had a lot of fun. But through that entire process, I kept my grand vision top of mind. I looked at every new experience as a chance to gain a skill that would serve me once I got to launch my company.

LEARN FROM YOUR FAILURES

I know. It's so common, it's a cliché: we learn from our failures. As with many cliches it contains a seed of truth, but it's also misleading. It implies that learning is a passive experience. A more accurate saying would be that we learn from our failures if we force ourselves to. The only way to learn from a mistake is to own it, to hold yourself accountable and then reflect on how you could have done better. For that reason, in my business, I always hold myself accountable first.

For example, in the late 2000s, I experienced a string of failures. Each contained a lesson. The economic collapse that had started in 2007 only accelerated. More and more people lost their jobs, and with their jobs they lost their dental insurance. Even the people who kept their jobs lost dental insurance as companies scrambled to cut spending everywhere they could without laying off more people.

I didn't pay myself the entire first year I owned my offices. I instead lived off the $70,000 I had saved. And then in 2009, just after Christmas, I got a call from my bank. The payroll didn't clear. In the middle of the holidays, I had to run out and transfer $25,000 from my personal savings into the payroll account to make sure my staff would get their checks. After that, I had less than $50,000 to my name. I remember driving home from the bank with knots in my stomach. I felt small and irrelevant. I kept thinking I would have to close the practices, declare bankruptcy, and go back to working as a dental associate.

This was the closest I've ever come to rock bottom. In many ways, the biggest lesson I learned from this experience had nothing to do with the mechanics of running a business. I mostly learned that I never wanted to feel like that again. I still remember the despair and frustration, and I carry it with me wherever I go. It's a little fire that burns inside me. It fuels me, and I protect it, I almost cherish it, so I can keep finding the motivation to push farther. I recommend that you and other aspiring entrepreneurs do the same when faced with a failure.

I stayed the course. We made some tweaks to the business, which I will describe in detail later on, that allowed it to become profitable and grow. By 2010, the office I had founded was finally starting to generate revenue, and the office I had acquired became profitable. I had found my footing. It was tenuous, sure, but I could stand.

Naturally, I decided it was time to take another huge risk and bought my fourth office. This one immediately backfired. It turned out to be a money pit. To break even, each office needed to gross about $40,000 a month. Several months in, the fourth office brought in only about $10,000.

Almost everyone in my life, even the people I knew and loved the most, questioned my decision. My wife, who I love dearly and who has supported me through this entire process, argued that I should sell that office. My mother would call and ask why I couldn't just be happy with a few offices, make some money, pay off my debt, and live a calm life. Despite my best efforts to keep my mind focused on the big picture, doubts crept in. The first offices hadn't taken this long to become profitable. Maybe my vision was just too grand.

I reasoned that I owed it to myself and my staff to at least try. As a first step, I spent more time at the location, observing work for a few days and interviewing the staff. Weirdly, everybody thought that business was good, if not booming. They felt they were doing their jobs well, and on the surface they were right. The front office people answered the phones and booked a steady stream of appointments. Hygienists and dental assistants executed their tasks quickly with a high degree of skill and professionalism. The dentists finished all the cleanings they needed to and received glowing reviews from guests. Yet each month we hemorrhaged money.

The office obviously was bursting with potential, I just needed to figure out how to unlock it.

During this process I realized the office struggled in two connected areas: efficiency and conversion. Efficiency is simply how quickly we can clean, diagnose, and treat our guests. Conversion measures the percentage of guests who come for cleanings and also receive necessary treatment. At Ideal Dental, we want every patient to have the chance to receive the care they need when they get diagnosed. We just think this is better for our guests. It saves them time and prevents them from having to rearrange their schedules to make a second visit. Most dentists cannot do this because they have not designed an efficient enough scheduling system to allow them to clean, diagnose, and treat everyone on the same day.

My first three offices operated with tremendous efficiency and had high conversion rates. This office operated more like a traditional dentist's office than an Ideal Dental branch, which was, by the way, entirely my fault. In each of the first three offices I had put in months of work on the front end. I'd personally trained and supervised each employee, and ensured they adopted our system before I moved on. For the fourth office, I hadn't done that and had assumed the staff would pick up the system with less oversight. I learned a valuable lesson here: True scale is when a business can grow without you. It was clear that I hadn't reached that point yet, and I needed to figure out how to get there.

> ***True scale is when a business can grow without you.***

For the next month, I worked exclusively in the struggling office. I went over every single process with every single employee. I showed the front office staff how to schedule appointments in the most effective way. I taught the hygienists and dental assistants how to set everything up. Most importantly, I worked with the dentist. He had been shy about asking people to have additional work done on the same day he saw them either because he had another appointment soon after that one, or because he didn't want to run behind. I reminded him that nobody visits the dentist on a whim. They come in because they recognize the importance of oral health. Usually, patients prefer same-day treatments, as it saves them another trip. It's as convenient for them as it for us. I worked with him until he got comfortable using the time in his schedule to treat patients the same day as their diagnosis.

By the time I left that office, it had gone from losing $30,000 a month to a $1,000-a-month profit, without letting go of a single employee. In each subsequent month, that office did better and better. Five years later, the office had an enterprise value of approximately $4 million.

All of this was possible only because I took responsibility for the office's failure. Many owners in my position would have charged into the office and threatened to let go of everyone if they didn't boost revenue. Or they might have declared the office a lost cause and sold it. Instead, I looked to myself first. I asked, "How have I failed to support this office?"

I went to the office not to bully people into giving me results, but to learn from them and get an accurate sense of the situation. This taught me that in order to scale I needed to devise a way to make sure each office followed the exact same processes. In this case it was in the early days, and I was able to take a full month to bring one outpost up to snuff. But I knew that as I continued to grow, that level of commitment would become impossible. I realized that if I wanted to scale, I would need to make sure I developed a robust training procedure so I could replicate my system with minimal effort.

You will likely face similar setbacks. The only way to overcome them is to be honest with yourself, admit your failures, and ask yourself—what can you do to be better? Remember, life is not a race, and you only fail when you give up on an idea or vision.

YOU WILL MAKE SACRIFICES

Growing up, I was hardly exceptional. I was an average student, an average athlete, and a rather average-looking guy. In my opinion, I wouldn't say that I'm particularly smart or talented. My one major advantage is that I am willing to make huge sacrifices and consistently work harder than anyone else in pursuit of my grand vision. And I maintain that level of dedication. In my experience, for most of us, it usually takes at least ten years of hard work, dedication, and unwavering commitment and sacrifice to be successful at anything.

In fact, by merely deciding to pursue my grand vision, I sacrificed the stability and relatively relaxed schedule most dentists enjoy. In the early days, I worked constantly—on weekends, through holidays, sometimes for sixteen hours a day. After I had kids, I had to spend time at home with them. I didn't party. Every free moment I had, I poured into the business. Pursuing a grand vision in any field requires this degree of dedication.

Beyond giving up activities that might be fun, pursuing a grand vision requires you find the resilience and fortitude to work through the challenges that life brings. For example, in the summer of 2010 when Ideal Dental was just a few struggling offices and I still couldn't pay myself, my mom got diagnosed with cancer. Just after lunch on a Friday, my fiancée called me with the news. When I hung up with my fiancée, I immediately got a call from my mother. When I hung up, I sat at my desk in the nearly empty office, shocked. I felt such an intense swirl of emotions that for a moment it almost didn't feel like anything at all.

I had a guest coming in a few minutes—my next appointment of the day—and it was just a cleaning. No real dental work, nothing pressing, something a hygienist usually does. But I had agreed to do it because during that time we couldn't afford a hygienist.

I considered explaining to my patient what had just happened and asking if we could reschedule. I didn't know if I could focus on the job and perform my best. I wanted to grieve, to go home, see my fiancée, cry. I wanted to call my mother. I was in shock—I couldn't for a second imagine a world without my mother.

I once read a saying that goes something like "When you lose your father, you become a man. When you lose your mother, you become an orphan." I felt that I was about to be orphaned. For my entire life, my mother had been there with me. She felt like a security blanket covering me. I got so much of my perseverance from her, not merely because she showed me how to keep going through difficult times, but also because on some level I genuinely believed I would always be safe as long as she was in this world.

As I processed these emotions, the patient walked in. I remembered that I had made a commitment to him. So I brought him to the examination room. I carefully washed my hands, put on my gloves, then strapped a surgical mask around my ears. I introduced myself and made polite small talk while adjusting the powerful overhead light. It took all my effort to maintain my peppy bedside demeanor. Finally, I asked him to open up. Lifting the scraper and mirror, I examined his teeth, prodded little divots that might have been cavities. In his mouth, everything was OK. Scraping away the tartar, I tried to focus as much as possible on the task in front of me. But as I fell into the familiar rhythm of scraping and rinsing, the dam I'd built around my emotions faltered. I sobbed silently beneath my mask. A seemingly endless stream of tears ran down my face.

By the time the patient left, I was exhausted and my mask was sopping wet.

Of course, if I had cancelled this appointment, it wouldn't have derailed my business. In all likelihood, we still would have grown to be as successful as we are. But we might not have, not because losing one appointment would have ruined us, but because my decision to cancel might have indicated that I lacked the necessary commitment and discipline to succeed.

I had promised my patient that I would personally take care of him. And I had promised myself that I would do everything possible to succeed. I had to follow through on those promises no matter what. My willingness to do so reverberates through the organization. I didn't make a big show out of that cleaning, but some people in that office knew what I was going through and saw how I handled it. The core conceit of my business was that I was asking people to go the extra mile for our customers. I knew if I had any hope of succeeding, I needed to lead by example. No matter what, there is a moment for everyone when life punches you in the face. The question is how you respond. Do you back down? Or is your conviction in your grand vision strong enough to keep you moving through the pain? This was one of the most defining moments in my journey.

People obsess over finding a work-life balance. But to be extremely successful, you must go through times of imbalance. There will be days when your work will need to matter more than your family, your feelings, your comfort. But then, once you have achieved success, you can find moments of balance. I have been fortunate to grow my business enough that I can take time off work without worrying. I can take my children on vacations. I can make it to their sports games and go to their parent-teacher conferences. And they know that all my work was in part for them, so I could offer them opportunities I'd never dreamed of. Yet, even after all the success, I still find myself at times being completely imbalanced and skewing more toward work or life. Work-life balance, in my opinion, is a term that applies to people who want to conform to societal norms. Ask any successful person, and they will share that you have to be imbalanced to achieve greatness and that sacrifices need to be made.

YOU'LL BEFRIEND FEAR

In 2022, I admitted to my friend, a self-made billionaire, that even though I had achieved a great deal, I still felt insecure. This was a revelation that I'd wanted to get off my chest for a while. It bothered me because I used to believe that once I achieved a certain degree of success, I would be able to calm down.

His response surprised me. He told me that he felt the same way. This was by all accounts one of the most successful people in the world. I was dismayed. He'd been in business twenty years longer than I had, and he still felt insecure? Would it ever end?

Then he said, "But that lingering insecurity is why we are both where we are today."

He helped me articulate something I'd felt for a long time. Fear will never ever go away. No matter how successful I became, every time I took a new risk and every time my company grew, I felt a spike of anxiety. Even in the (brief) moments that Ideal Dental held more or less steady, I worried that everything would suddenly collapse. It's like the trace amounts of radiation from the sun that we all live with at all times of every day.

Since fear never disappears, especially for people who pursue a grand vision, your best option is to learn to befriend fear. Let it guide you. You feel fear most when you leave your comfort zone and grow. So if a new challenge or a new idea makes you anxious, it's a good sign that it's at least a seed of something worth doing. Then you can harness the energy that fear creates to achieve new heights. Every day since 2009, when I had to use my personal funds to cover payroll, I've been terrified of ever being in that position again. By 2013, I was married, and my wife and I had just welcomed our first son, Daniel, into the world. I wanted to provide for them. The business was better, but I couldn't let go of my lingering anxiety. I focused my anxious energy on growing the business. Since then, I've used that memory of what it felt like that winter morning, covering payroll from my limited savings, to keep me focused on doing whatever it takes to never end up in that position again. That feeling has stayed with me; it drives me every day and also keeps me humble.

One of the most fear-inducing steps you have to make comes early. Eventually, to keep growing you will need to stop working *in* the business and start working *on* the business. This is a massive shift that almost always requires a slight dip in income. For example, as a practicing dentist, I made $200,000 a year. When I transitioned to working on the business, my income dropped to $80,000 because I was seeing fewer patients. I knew if things went well, my income would balloon well beyond $200,000 a year. But I also knew that if we went south, I'd end up back where I was, just with a lot more debt.

One of the most fear-inducing steps you have to make comes early. Eventually, to keep growing you will need to stop working **in** *the business and start working* **on** *the business.*

Giving up that dependable $200,000 was scary. That was good money, enough to buy a nice house, support my family, and go on vacations. But by working on the business, I reached a point where I was bringing in great money, having a much larger impact on the world, and able to afford an even better lifestyle. In the end, the best antidote to fear is to make up your mind that the chance at greatness outweighs the guaranteed good—not to mention its impact on the lives of your team members that join you for this journey. It won't make the fear go away, but it will make it all worthwhile.

YOUR GRAND VISION WILL GROW WITH YOU

As I continued to grow and evolve, so did my grand vision, particularly after 2020. From that point, my vision evolved along two major vectors of energy. The first was something of a continuation of my original vision but taken to its logical extreme. The second was a pivot, as much as possible, to enabling other people.

For context, this had come shortly after I made a financing deal with Blackstone, the world's largest alternative asset manager, with $1 trillion in an AUM. It was never ever about the money for me, but this deal still represented a watershed moment in my career. By just about any entrepreneurial standard, a deal with Blackstone essentially meant that I had made it. Ideal Dental's future, at that point, seemed as secure as anything in business can be. Strategizing for, and even working at, Ideal Dental took less time and energy from me so I could reflect and think about what sort of legacy I wanted to leave. That and working with Blackstone gave me access to resources and connections on a scale that I had never dreamed of.

In my reflection, I discovered that I wanted to do whatever I could to empower other people, to help them grow, to help them achieve their own dreams. In many key ways this didn't actually represent a departure from my previous grand vision or my previous way of operating. I had already considered my role as a CEO to be, first and foremost, enabling the people I worked with. I offered support, I listened to people's goals, and I tried to put them in positions to succeed. But during this period of reflection, I also realized that because of the new relationship with

Blackstone, I was now able to help people more than ever before. This book is a part of that effort.

The second part of that effort was to create within Ideal Dental a joint venture model. A joint venture model is similar to a franchise model in that I give dentists the option to buy into Ideal Dental and own and operate their own location of the brand. This model has several benefits. It allows us to expand more quickly with less risk. Instead of raising all the capital, our joint venture investors contribute their own capital. More importantly, though, it allows me to help hundreds of people build their own independent wealth. They get to partially own their own business while leveraging the trust that Ideal Dental's national brand generates.

The deal with Blackstone also enabled me to pursue new business ventures. The first one I launched was a direct offshoot of my original grand vision. I wanted to be the Starbucks of dentistry, and I almost entirely achieved this goal. There was one last major area for me to grow into.

When you walk into Starbucks, you don't just get to buy coffee to go. They have a whole range of other products: coffee mugs (often themed according to city), French presses, little bags of cookies or chocolate-covered graham crackers, bags of coffee, to-go mugs, and a whole host of prepackaged healthy snacks and chilled beverages. Some of these they stock through partnerships with other companies such as Oatly oat milk. But Starbucks manufactures many of these products themselves. Regardless of the source, when Starbucks puts it in their stores, they endorse the product.

At Ideal Dental, we also have dental products in our offices. Like most dentists, we give clients a little take-home bag with hygiene items such as floss, a new toothbrush, and toothpaste. And because we give them away, our clients often assume that those are the products we endorse. But that's not the case. We only give the products away for free because we get them as free samples from the manufacturer. Whenever my patients asked me if I used the toothpaste or toothbrush I just gave them, I didn't know what to say. The honest answer is no. I, like any other dentist I know, use an electric toothbrush instead of the two-buck disposable ones we put in the giveaway bags. Likewise, many of those toothpastes, and many of the ones people buy in drug stores, contain peroxide or other powerful bleaching and whitening agents. While those ingredients work to remove stains, they're so powerful they also damage enamel.

Giving away these products had always bothered me because I felt I wanted to have a better option for my clients. So I decided to launch my own oral care product line called ToothScience. This line uses higher-quality ingredients in its toothpaste, and manufactures clinician-tested-and-approved products that consistently clean without damaging enamel and while preventing cavities. We also shy away from the gaudy branding of other oral care lines and opt for a sleek, modern look: black lettering on a white background. It matches our no-nonsense commitment to quality and science-based decision-making.

Finally, I let my vision evolve beyond dentistry, and in doing so I found a way to bring a part of my motherland to my new home. My parents are Pakistani, and the most important sport where they come from is cricket, which is also huge in Zimbabwe. I grew up playing the sport, the second most popular in the world behind soccer. I loved it, but when I came to the United States, cricket was nowhere to be found. That all changed in the summer of 2023 when Major League Cricket was launched in the States. In the years leading up to the launch of the league, I decided to become an investor in one of the teams, the Texas Super Kings. The captain of that team, Faf du Plessis, is South African. When I met him, we bonded about what it was like to grow up in southern Africa, shared stories from our childhoods, and reflected on what an incredible experience it was to bring an activity so important to us to a new country.

YOU WILL CHANGE PEOPLE'S LIVES

Thousands of times every day, people come through Ideal Dental offices and leave happier than they were when they arrived. Our guests leave in less pain and more confident in their health. And our employees leave full of purpose and buoyed by the joy of a job well done. But more than that, we have helped countless families economically. I'm on a personal mission to resuscitate the flagging American dream. We pay our employees well above the standard industry rates. We ensure they can grow and advance in our company. We even share ownership with some of our workers. We give equity as a bonus, essentially sweat equity for people who we see are going above and beyond. We offer other high performers a chance to invest directly and buy part of the company. We don't limit this to our founding staff or to the top executives. Anyone—any doctor, office manager, front office staff—who performs well gets this opportunity. A lot of them take advantage, and when we went through our second round of private capitalization, it resulted in about $50 million being paid out to employees.

After our second finance deal, I wanted to expand the pathways for employees to build their own wealth. To do so, we created what's called a joint venture option. We were opening about forty locations a year, and we offered new dentists the chance to buy a large stake—about 45 percent—in a new office. This is close to a franchise model, where we still own a stake in the location and provide the branding, advertising, and operational instructions, but the practicing dentists own a part of the office. That's a path to real wealth, created for hundreds of people and their families. Our company has been the tide to lift all these ships, and yours can be too.

You Can Succeed Beyond Your Wildest Dreams

When I created the holding company for Ideal Dental, I decided to call it DECA Dental. *DECA* because at that time my goal was to have ten offices. I figured if I could get to ten, then I would have proof that this might work. The vision was always larger than that, though. When I launched the website, I included an office locator map that showed the entire world even though we were just in Dallas because I hoped to one day reach the world. But at the time, I wasn't even sure we'd reach ten offices. Now we have over 150 open locations, with another fifty being developed and built. I'm able to impact people's lives on a scale I never thought possible and to use my position to start new ventures and help other people grow and achieve their own dreams.

The most miraculous part is that it keeps going. We all have billions of dreams. It's great when you get to achieve them. But its more amazing to reach a place you haven't dreamed of yet.

CHAPTER TWO

Know Your Customer

In the style of a famous John F. Kennedy quote—ask not what your business can do for you; ask what you can do for your business. Far too many entrepreneurs fall into the trap of viewing their business through the lens of their own desires, not the customer's. When they do that, they make decisions that help themselves instead of developing a system or a product that maximizes customer satisfaction.

There's nothing wrong with using your business to pursue your dreams. As I've said, the desire to execute a grand vision is an integral part of success. But to succeed, the grand vision must focus on, and prioritize the needs of, the customer before addressing the founder's needs. Ultimately, if you're not fulfilling a need or improving a process, you're not creating value. And value creation is rewarded.

Every world-changing company achieved success because it provided something that a consumer wanted better than anyone had before. Another way to describe this is that every great company found a gap in the market they could fill better than any competitor. Amazon offered legendary customer service, a generous return policy, everything you could imagine to buy (even live insects!) in one place, and shipping faster than anything we had seen before. Whole Foods offered, well, whole, organic foods. Amazon didn't reach its position because founder Jeff Bezos wanted to one day become the richest person in the world, but because Bezos never forgot about the customer, even famously leaving an empty seat at the table in any meeting he held to represent the customer.

Look at my own industry: dentistry. It's been around forever, and for the bulk of the last fifty years, it has more or less been practiced the same way. That modus operandi was designed by dentists, for dentists. All I did was develop a customer-centric model and then figure out how to scale that model. As a small example, take business hours. Most dental offices are only open Monday through Thursday because the dentist who works there enjoys three-day weekends. But dental emergencies don't stop just because dentists stop working, so I decided to open our offices six days a week. It's a small tweak but one that makes us far more convenient for our customers and proves that we care more about serving our guests than we do about getting in eighteen holes on Friday morning.

Keep in mind that not every gap is worth pursuing, and trying to chase after every gap will dilute your brand and siphon vital energy away from your key initiatives. In my experience, the gaps worth filling usually meet three main criteria. First, they correspond to a customer's currently unaddressed need. Second, filling that gap is in alignment with your business's core competency, vision, and values. Third, filling the gap has the potential to increase profits, either because a large portion of the population needs it, or because it is so specialized or fantastic that the niche market that does need it will pay a premium to have it.

So what differentiator can you create in your customers' experience to give you a competitive edge? Here are a few places to look. In my experience, customers have three types of concerns: those related to time, money, and fear. If you can solve all three, you will succeed.

TIME

Time factors simply into a customer's decision-making process: they want convenience and efficiency—the best possible product or service in the fastest possible time. There's nothing more annoying than having to wait in a long line or drive from store to store or waste hours on hold with a customer service representative. Entire business empires have been built around convenience. Uber has succeeded because they made it possible to call a car to almost any part of any city, and to get food from just about any area restaurant.

The key to efficiency is to find and relentlessly attack the most common sources of pain for your customer, client, or patient related to time. At Ideal Dental, we made several innovations that dramatically improved convenience for our guests. The first had to do with scheduling, which traditionally caused several pain points. Like most dental offices, the dental office where I completed my associateship often scheduled as many patients as possible each day, without building in room between appointments. The logic behind this was simple: it allowed doctors to see as many patients as possible, and since most dental offices frequently deal with cancellations, they could use time freed up by cancelled appointments for added flexibility.

While it might have seemed like a good idea from the dentist's perspective, in practice, the system eliminated flexibility, and often led to huge delays and chaos. If even one appointment ran over, or one patient showed up late, the whole the rest of the day could be thrown off schedule, as these issues and overruns tend to compound. One overrun appointment delays the assistant from sterilizing and prepping the room ahead of the next patient, which delays seating the next patient, which causes the hygienist to fall behind, which delays X-rays and the dentist, which causes more late appointments, which . . . you get the idea.

In my three years of working as a dental associate, I can't remember a single day where we ran on schedule. Even if we had, the system we used had built in other inefficiencies. For one, it prevented us from accepting walk-ins, which often forced us to either send away patients experiencing severe pain or an emergency, or schedule an appointment for them well into the future. Second, it prevented us from performing same-day care. Often, we would do the cleaning and X-rays and discover that someone needed a crown or a filling or a root canal. The patient would ask if we could do it the same day, and we'd have to tell them no because we didn't have the time. This would force them to take more time off work to receive a treatment that we should have been able to do right away. To make matters worse, sometimes patients would miss that appointment, further delaying important medical care.

This flummoxed me. What other industry works like that? Imagine going to Nordstrom, finding a shirt you like, and then when you try to buy it, they say, "Actually, we need to hold that on the rack for another two months, can you come back then?"

To prevent this absurd scenario, at Ideal Dental we made three major innovations. First, we developed a new scheduling system. Instead of booking every guest one on top of the other, we scheduled in enough flex time to be able to provide any necessary treatment for every guest. In my mind, it was OK for a dentist to have some slack in their schedule but unacceptable for a patient to have to wait. Second, we kept a few slots open each day that allowed us to either handle walk-ins or to catch up if we fell behind. Third, we set strict time limits on each part of the guest experience from how long a guest should wait (no more than five minutes) to how long a cleaning, X-rays, and each and every procedure should take.

Then we built a computer system that tracked our actual results against our goals and used that data in our performance evaluation system.

This won't be the first time I say this: if these solutions seem simple, that's because they are. The secret to business success often rests in simple, easy-to-execute plans that deliver what people want.

The other major pain point I uncovered was that the office I worked for, like most dental offices, was closed Friday through Sunday. This is one of the most egregious examples of a businessperson thinking about their needs before the needs of the customer. Many dentists like to play golf on Fridays, and many of them only work four days a week because they can. It makes sense, sure. But they provide healthcare. When I was a dental associate, patients frequently called on a Thursday complaining about pain. I would want to see them right away, but I couldn't.

> ***The secret to business success often rests in simple, easy-to-execute plans that deliver what people want.***

I'm not saying that every single dentist should work six or even five days a week. But it doesn't make sense to close an entire office for three days a week. I remember one client in particular who called on a Thursday afternoon in severe pain. All I could do was prescribe some pain medication and tell him to come in on Monday. Over the weekend, his pain got worse and worse. He couldn't find a single dentist who would see him. Desperate, he eventually went to the ER. They had to pull the tooth. If he had come in earlier, say on that Thursday, I likely could have saved his tooth. I witnessed countless examples of this, where people were forced into a costly, painful, and ultimately preventable procedure because they couldn't get a weekend appointment.

As such, many Ideal Dental branches are open on Saturdays and have a six-days-a-week model. We do close on Sundays—people need a break, and one day's wait rarely leads to dire medical outcomes. This was one of our most successful innovations and helped us win over a lot of early customers. For example, in about 2010 when we had three offices, we got a call on a Saturday morning from a woman with a chipped tooth. She was getting married that night, and they had wedding party photos booked that afternoon at 2 PM. Her tooth had been chipped since that Thursday, and she had been calling her dentist and any other dentist she could find, but none had been able to give her an appointment. In fact, she'd hardly been able to get on the phone with an assistant.

She found us that Saturday, and we scheduled her within the hour that she'd called. I installed a temporary replacement for her chipped tooth, so she would look like herself in her photographs, while we waited for the lab to make the permanent fix. She thanked us effusively. She made us her new primary dentist. Pretty soon, her husband, parents, in-laws, and, eventually, even her new kids all became our patients. But most importantly, we helped her enjoy a momentous day.

Finally, I also changed how we handle closing times. When I worked as an associate, I would frequently receive a call about ten or fifteen minutes before close, usually from a patient in significant pain asking if they could come in that day. That office's policy was to refuse and not to stay open late. When I started Ideal Dental and was working in our offices, whenever we got that kind of call, I offered to stay late and see the patient. Usually, one or two other employees would see my willingness to make that sacrifice and offer to do the same. Obviously, because they worked late, I paid them overtime. I also got in the habit of bringing in a breakfast treat the next morning for those employees who'd stayed. Before long, other dentists started to follow my lead and offer to stay a little later to help a guest out of pain. As we scaled, this became standard practice across all our outposts. Of course, if people have to leave at the close of business to pick up their kids or something like that, then we understand. But luckily, it doesn't take a large staff to run a dental office for one patient, so we usually have enough volunteers to make it work.

There are countless examples of companies succeeding because they manage to streamline an inefficient industry. A great example is health food. For decades, almost every quick-service restaurant brand pedaled highly processed fatty fried food. Those foods are the easiest to ship and the quickest to make en masse. Frozen french fries never expire. Dehydrated refried beans take up negligible space in a shipping container. A burger can stay "fresh" for an hour under a heating lamp. A limited number of fresh fruits and vegetables simplifies supply chains. Instead of worrying about getting enough fresh, local-ish vegetables, most fast-food chains just need bags of iceberg lettuce and presliced tomatoes and onions.

This dynamic created a gap, especially as Americans became more health conscious. Any company that could figure out how to offer quick, tasty, and healthy food could grow rapidly. In the late 2010s through the early 2020s, we saw several national brands emerge to fill this gap. Restaurants like Sweetgreen and Dig offer salads and grain-based bowls with freshly prepared vegetables and proteins. Sweetgreen, in particular, has sought as many ways as possible to offer healthy food quickly and cheaply. For starters, they partner with over a hundred individual farms and suppliers, keeping them as hyperlocal as possible. For example, a location in New York City will likely receive most of its greens and vegetables from farms in New York, Massachusetts, and Vermont. Each location keeps a chalkboard at the front of the store that tracks where the ingredients come from.

While this hyperlocal approach does have some downsides—it requires restaurants to maintain relationships with far more suppliers—it offers myriad benefits. More local ingredients mean shorter shipping routes and lowered costs. It also allows restaurants to restock more frequently and easily, so they can reduce food waste by ordering only what their product-use algorithms say they'll need in the next several days.

During the peak of the COVID-19 pandemic, more customers turned en masse to digital ordering to reduce their exposure risk, a trend that shows little signs of reversing. Sweetgreen adapted to this change early. They added a second line completely dedicated to online orders—and enough employees to staff it—to every store. This way, in-person customers wouldn't have to wait longer for service. They also added prefab shelving at the front of the store where completed and paid for orders could await pickup, so customers could get in, get their food, and get out without interrupting an employee's work.

In another time-saving move, they changed their ticket and receipt design to improve accuracy and efficiency. Instead of merely listing the name of the signature salad a customer ordered, the receipts now list each ingredient in the salad. This means that the line cook can use the order ticket as a reference and doesn't have to rely on memory or out-of-the-way recipe placards.

Finally, Sweetgreen built an algorithm that automatically generates a cooking schedule that keeps a steady stream of steaming-hot sweet potatoes, chicken, quinoa, and rice flowing to the line. The algorithm incorporates environmental data—like the kitchen's temperature and humidity—as well as customer behavior data—like the number of visits they usually get a certain time on a Monday and which dishes have been the most popular. It also considers the employees' schedules and rotations to assign the task of cooking new batches to whichever employee is not on the line at a given time. This makes everything more efficient and reduces waste because trays of prepared but unused ingredients don't need to be discarded. That keeps costs down and helps Sweetgreen deliver delicious and healthy meals quickly.

MONEY

Money. For many customers, this is the most important consideration. *How much will this cost? Do I need it? Can I afford it? How can I afford it?*

If you operate in an industry that has reached what is called commodity status—in other words, any industry with minimal differentiators between companies other than price (for example, fast food, basic cybersecurity software, literal commodities like oil and gas)—then what matters most is finding a way to offer your product or service at the cheapest possible rate. However, since you're reading this book, you probably work in a harder-to-scale, higher-skill-level service industry (for example, dentistry, law, physical therapy, consulting). By definition, these industries are more difficult to standardize and therefore less likely to reach commodity status. Thus, for our purposes, the goal isn't to charge customers as little as possible. In fact, if you offer highly specialized elite services to wealthy clients (as McKinsey and Company, the world's foremost management consulting firm does) or services covered by insurance (like dentistry), then charging too little can damage your business. Your services have a certain value, and high-ticket customers will expect to spend large sums to see significant results. Likewise, if most of your clients have insurance, then what you bill hardly matters. Insurance will likely have a cap on what they pay through a co-pay or deductible. In these situations, what matters most is how you talk about price, not the price itself.

Money issues induce more stress for more people than anything else in the modern world. If you can make conversations around price as comfortable and pleasant as possible, it will bolster customer satisfaction and drive sales. To do this, I follow one guiding principle in designing my company's policies: make customers feel cared for, not squeezed. In fact, it's so integral to my philosophy, I call it the Ahmed Doctrine.

The Ahmed Doctrine

In 1970 the American economist Milton Friedman laid out a philosophy that would dominate business practices for at least the next fifty years. He argued that each business was beholden only to its shareholders or owners, and that their primary purpose was to generate as much profit as possible. This idea became known as the Friedman Doctrine. It was taught in the world's leading business schools, and was even adopted by the Business Roundtable, a lobbying group comprised of the leaders of the largest companies in the world, as the official Statement on the Purpose of a Corporation.

I run my business according to what I call the Ahmed Doctrine, which states that the primary purpose of any company is to put the customer's well-being before all else. The beautiful thing is that any company that truly excels at the Ahmed Doctrine will, on account of their superior service, generate profits naturally.

While the original Friedman Doctrine had many issues, one of the major problems was that it could incentivize a deeply unpleasant customer experience. Defenders of Friedman argue that the best way to grow profits is to provide the best product, and there is some truth to that. But another way to grow profits is to try to squeeze as much money out of each customer as possible; manipulate market conditions to create a functional monopoly (as many internet service providers have); or reduce costs by selling lower-quality products or cutting staff or both and therefore provide worse customer service.

When companies chase profits in these ways, people often end up feeling less like a customer and more like a mark. If you've ever paid $7 for a water bottle in an airport or $15 for a beer at a sporting event, then you know what I mean.

By 2019, business leaders had begun to shift away from Friedman's doctrine, and the Business Roundtable updated their statement accordingly. As of 2022, the Statement on the Purpose of a Corporation now claims that companies have a responsibility to customers, employees, and the communities they operate in, as well as to shareholders. Still, far too many businesses fall into the trap of prioritizing profit above all else.

Perhaps the industries in the best position to try to squeeze money out of customers are those that provide a genuine necessity such as gas, housing, or healthcare. At Ideal Dental, our guiding philosophy has always been to assuage as much concern about cost as possible and to make people recognize that we don't see them as giant dollar signs in our operating chairs, but as guests with needs that we must meet.

These people who come to see us are often already a little bit nervous about whatever dental concern brought them to us in the first place. Then they often worry that their insurance will refuse to cover whatever treatment they need. Or they might not have any insurance at all, and they've come in because they've been delaying going to the dentist, only to suffer increasing amounts of pain until they had no choice but to come see us.

We go to great lengths to handle the money conversation with as much grace and dignity as possible. To start, we make sure to listen to what each guest tells us about their needs and relationship to their teeth. I could probably find at least one thing to correct in every single person in America's mouth. For some people, it would be genuine health concerns—root canals, fillings, a mouth guard to prevent enamel loss from teeth grinding. For others, it would be cosmetic fixes—teeth whitening, repairing minor chips, straightening teeth.

To maximize our profits, we could train our dentists to give people the hard sell on the new teeth-whitening program or adult braces or whatever. But that would feel pushy and ultimately erode trust. Instead, we treat our relationship with our guests as a partnership. We ask people what they're curious about, what hurts, and we prioritize medical necessities. If we do notice a cosmetic issue that would be remedied by a quick fix, we bring it up. If the person isn't interested, then we drop it.

We've established a dedicated role called a financial coordinator in each of our offices. The financial coordinator learns everything they can about the cost of each procedure, what each type of insurance covers, and how financing options work, including who is likely to get approved and who isn't. Finally, the financial coordinator has the ability to, if necessary, work out an agreement with the patient. For example, after the doctor diagnoses the patient and describes what sort of work is needed, the financial coordinator comes in and says something like, "The dentist thinks you need a crown. The total cost is $1,000, and your insurance will cover $700 of that. That leaves your out-of-pocket cost at $300. Would you like to get started today?"

If the patient says yes, that's great, it's done. If the patient says no, then we go through a couple of other options. The first is third-party financing. The financial coordinator will check to make sure the patient is approved. If they are, great; if not, then the financial coordinator has an option to work with the client directly. For example, if the procedure requires two days of work, then we ask if they can pay half up front and the other half when we complete the work. If it's a one-day operation, we find a similar solution—such as half now and half in a month, or half now and half at next cleaning.

There have even been times, though they are rare, when we offer people pro bono services. This usually happens when someone comes in with a dental emergency in pain, and they need the tooth pulled right away. If they come in like that, they most likely had been neglecting their dental care, probably because they were uninsured and couldn't afford consistent checkups and other preventative care. In those cases, we offer to pull the tooth for free. This does a couple of things: It reenforces to everyone working for us just how important our work is. It shows them we are willing to put our mission—helping patients—above pure concern for profit. It also breeds goodwill within the community, which sometimes, though not always, yields a direct return on investment.

Then we do everything we can to make our product affordable without impacting our bottom line, especially in times of economic hardship. For example, the 2009 recession.

In a strange way, this financial meltdown may have ended up helping our business. When people lost their insurance and their jobs and reduced their spending, many stopped going to the dentist for checkups and cleanings. If they did come in, they would hesitate to get any work done unless they were in extreme pain. I could understand this position completely—at the same time I was asking myself how I could possibly stay afloat. I hadn't paid myself, and I was doing dentistry out of two offices while also trying to learn how to attract new customers, hire well, and do everything else it took to run a business.

We couldn't wait for the economy to rebound to the point where people could come back in like they used to, so we developed a way to make our services more affordable. We rolled out the Metrocare Dental Plan for uninsured guests. This was essentially in-house dental insurance. This plan offered guests a free cleaning and a free initial exam when they came in, and then discounted out-of-pocket rates. We essentially offered them the option to pay us what most insurance companies would pay out for any given procedure (which is often substantially less than what we bill them for), all for a small flat annual fee. We marketed it by saying: "Eventually most people need dental care. We want you to come in earlier, so we can catch any problems before they get worse. A filling or a new cap on a tooth might cost $200. If you don't get that in time, you might very well be looking at a root canal, and those cost $2,000."

It proved to be incredibly popular and still is. As of 2022, about 80 percent of our customers are insured, 12 percent of our patients use our Metrocare plan, and the rest pay out of pocket.

Finally, we make sure to protect our patients' privacy regarding money more than our competitors do. I've seen dental offices and have talked to dentists who work in offices where patients can hear everything that happens in a neighboring operatory, or where dentists leave the door open when talking about money. This feels disrespectful, and, intentionally or not, seems to pressure people into saying yes to something. Who wants to announce to an entire dentist's office that they can't afford a $300 co-pay? We keep the conversations quiet, behind closed doors, and usually have music or a TV program playing (both in the lobby and in the operatory) to mask the voices. Small practices like these make customers feel safe, protected, and keep them coming back.

FEAR

The last major factor in customer decision-making is fear. Fear operates according to a simple equation: when someone's fear of inaction is greater than their fear of action, they will buy. For example, people visit the dentist because they're more afraid of the negative health effects of missing appointments than of the pain associated with a procedure. It follows that to win customers, you can do one of two things: You can make them afraid not to work with you, what I call scare-tactic marketing. Or you can reduce their fear of working with you, what I call outcome-focused marketing.

As a positive person, I don't believe in scare-tactic marketing. Instead, at Ideal Dental we aim to reduce the fear potential by focusing on the outcomes we provide. Not only do I feel this is a more honest and positive approach, it's also more effective. This is because scare-tactic marketing, being negatively focused, tells people what to avoid but doesn't highlight what actions to take.

For example, a home security company might run ads about the rate of break-ins spiking in a certain area. But all that does is make the customer afraid of not having a home security system. It doesn't make an argument for why the customer should choose their specific home security system. Likewise, if we ran a bunch of ads with pictures of people with their teeth falling out, it would just make someone want to go to *a* dentist. Instead, we advertise how Ideal Dental's expanded hours, high-quality dentistry, and money-back guarantees lead to a more convenient and comfortable customer experience. In the long run, outcome-focused marketing builds trust and a large, loyal customer base that can fuel your growth.

Of course, the marketing is merely how you communicate your company's services to the world. The best marketing imaginable is completely worthless if you don't actually address customer fear. Here are three primary strategies to lower your customer's fear quotient: educate your customers, create a comfortable experience, and reduce customer risk.

EDUCATE YOUR CUSTOMERS

Uncertainty inspires fear. A lack of knowledge creates a feeling that you're not in control. How can someone know what route will be best for them or their family if they don't understand their options? This is particularly important in a service industry that requires specialized knowledge as with dentistry, law, or consulting. In those cases, not only is a customer already aware they haven't a clue, they don't even know what they don't know.

To close this gap, you need to educate your customers. Most companies try to do this, but they fail because they share their expertise with prospects and customers only in an attempt to convince them that they are, in fact, experts. This is little more than grandstanding. Actual education requires communicating your expertise in a way that the customer can comprehend. The goal should be for the customer to feel like a partner, to feel like they've got enough knowledge to make the right decisions.

At Ideal Dental, we train all our dentists and hygienists to describe in an understandable way the different health challenges people face with their teeth, and we leave plenty of time for the patient to ask follow-up questions. We also train employees to explain why regular checkups matter and that if guests wait until they feel pain to come in, they're probably waiting until it's too late for a simple fix.

Yet we discovered our most effective education method almost by accident. Our company's early years coincided with an explosion in the popularity of clear braces, an alternative form of braces fashioned from clear plastic. Designing clear braces requires a comprehensive 3D image of the mouth. We realized that the 3D images could also serve as an educational tool. It takes clinical training to properly read an X-ray, but anyone can interpret a 3D image. We take a scan of every guest's mouth, and it leads to an amazing result. People can actually see the decay in their teeth, the areas of their gums that are swollen and bleeding, or whatever problem they face. They no longer have to take a doctor's word that a blank spot where a tooth should be on an X-ray is tooth decay, they can actually see the decay. After this, armed with more knowledge than they had before, they can make informed decisions.

Other successful players in industries that inspire a lot of fear have employed a similar approach to great effect. For example, aviation. Millions of Americans rank flying and heights as among their most powerful phobias. With good reason. If something goes wrong on an airplane, it can have devastating consequences. To assuage these fears, the aviation industry takes several steps. First, they develop and abide by rigorous safety standards and build a tremendous degree of redundancy into their systems. According to studies of plane crashes through history, the crew and captain usually made seven consecutive errors before their aircraft went down.[1] Such a dedication to safety makes air travel in the United States and Europe significantly less risky than driving a car, a fact that most of us already know because the airlines do such a good job of educating us about how miraculously safe their products are.[2]

They go further still in their education efforts by teaching everyone who travels exactly what to do in the unlikely event of an emergency. Most frequent flyers can recite the safety announcement from memory. *Put on your mask before assisting others. Your life jacket is located under your seat. Pull the red tab to inflate. If the life vest does not inflate, use the tubes . . .*

You get the idea. It's important to remember that the delivery of this information plays a role in both how much people retain and how much they're calmed. For the most part, the days of an attendant droning on about seat belts and smoke detectors are gone. Some airlines have opted to shoot glossy informational videos with elaborate sets, clever camera work, and hordes of actors and extras. These look like a cross between a Wes Anderson film and something from a 1950s movie musical, and they're filled with small jokes, clever surprises, and enchanting visuals and choreography.

Others, like Southwest Airlines, one of the global leaders in customer service, allow flight attendants to turn the announcement into a stand-up comedy set. They make jokes about being selfish when putting on your mask before you help your child and jokingly scold people for not listening. This is brilliant, not merely because it helps ensure everyone pays attention, but because it also allows the attendants to show their unique personalities and to create an instant rapport and relationship with the entire cabin. Air travelers feel like they know a bit about who they've entrusted part of their safety to, and that can help them relax.

The bottom line is that both of the above approaches are fun. They amuse people (especially children) or mesmerize them, and they put the passengers at ease so they can enjoy one of the great wonders of contemporary society.

CREATE A COMFORTABLE EXPERIENCE

Certain industries inherently inspire more fear than others. For example, more people are afraid of flying than going to the movies. Therefore, the amount of effort you need to exert to keep customers calm depends on the industry you're in. Dentistry likely ranks as one of the most fear-inspiring professions even though it has one of the highest rates of consumer safety of any industry. To combat that fear, dental practices need to do what they can to make the experience comfortable for their guests.

Creating a comfortable experience starts with staff. I want people to feel comfortable from the moment they first call our offices until they are home and recovered from whatever procedure they needed. When we hire, we look for people who will sincerely empathize with the patients. We want people who understand that they help guests live healthier, happier lives. If you called most dentists at 4:45 complaining of severe tooth pain, they would prescribe some pain meds and tell you to come in the morning. We hire the type of people who ask, "How fast can you get here?" and then keep the office open past five to make sure that person gets care.

Then we go out of our way to build a comfortable experience in each office. We have multiple TVs in the waiting rooms and even have TVs and streaming services in each operatory so anxious patients can distract themselves with their favorite show.

Since we cater to families, we have to handle kids' fears too. Much of the fear that dentists inspire starts at childhood, but it doesn't have to.

We have games in the waiting room, and whenever a young child comes in, we make sure one of the TVs is playing an age-appropriate children's show. By creating a comfortable and fun environment for the kids, we also please the parents because they don't want their kids to be crying, in pain, nervous, or bored.

We train our doctors and hygienists to connect with kids and make them more comfortable. We start each appointment with giving kids a special mouthwash to swish around that makes all the plaque in their mouth glow purple. Then we have them look at themselves in the mirror. They marvel (or say something like *ew*) at their purple-mottled mouth. Then after their cleaning, we repeat the mouthwash process. They look at the mirror and see nothing but pearly whites. This isn't just fun, it also educates. They get to actually see the impact that brushing has on their teeth and understand how important it is for their overall health. We also introduce children to the tools we use for their cleaning, most importantly the dreaded scraper. We let them hold it, inspect it, and poke parts of their arm with it to show that while it looks like a nasty little hook, it's actually not too sharp. Then, when the exam is all done, we open up a big toy chest and let them pick something out to take home.

REDUCE CUSTOMER RISK

The more a customer risks when they enter a transaction, the more fear they feel. This is why buying a house causes more anxiety than picking up a new toaster, and why going in for surgery (oral or otherwise) causes more anxiety than a manicure. At the nail salon, the worst that can happen is a minor wound thanks to a mishandled nail clipper. In the operating room, mistakes can lead to costly follow-ups, painful complications, or death.

I knew that the risk of low-quality dentistry contributed to my guests' fears, so I set out to assure them that we only deliver the best care. In any healthcare field, this is no small feat. Different doctors have different skill levels. But my goal wasn't unprecedented. At that time, I saw a clear example in the healthcare space of a retail chain providing consistent results: pharmacies—namely CVS and Walgreens. Nobody ever worries that CVS will give them the wrong pills or the wrong dosages.

To become as standardized as possible, we did two main things. First, we guaranteed all the work we did. If we put in a crown and it fails within the first five years, we redo the procedure at no charge. Of course, to prevent losses from constant rework, we ensure that all our dentist hires have had top-notch training, we closely monitor everyone's performance, and we fire any dentist who makes too many mistakes.

Second, I made sure we had complete control over who staffed our offices. To do that, I decided to open as many offices from scratch as possible. When I acquired an existing office, I had to make changes beyond superficial things like the décor and the layout. I was also taking on some, if not all, of its staff, and that meant getting my new employees to buy into our culture. I asked dentists to go beyond the normal call of duty for their profession. Work on weekends. Call every single patient they put under to make sure they came out of the anesthetic OK. Dentists often resisted adapting from a dentist-centric model to the Ideal Dental system, and I often had to fire staff who didn't fit our culture. On the other hand, when I open an office from scratch, every dentist I hire knows exactly what they're signing up for when they apply.

The last major fear or risk I encountered was my own, and it dealt with guests asking for referrals. This request stems from fear, or at least a concern the patient has when they recognize they don't know where to find a competent specialist, so they look to their dentist for guidance. In the patient's eyes, a referral usually constitutes an endorsement. They assume their provider knows the specialist and can vouch for their work.

It would be a great system except that primary providers almost never know anything about the specialist they refer their patients to.

Every day as an associate, I referred people to specialists I didn't know at all. This enabled me to assuage my patients' fear but only through a process that felt deceitful. One day as I reflected on this issue, I recalled my first day at Tufts, watching all those hands go up and thinking it would be great to have each of those specialists working in the same location. I started to hire specialists to work in our offices, focusing first on the most common needs, orthodontists and oral surgeons. Even when we couldn't hire doctors to work directly in our office, I made it a policy to proactively research nearby specialists, so I could make referrals with confidence.

WHEN THINGS GO WRONG: TRANSPARENCY AND ACCOUNTABILITY

As much as we work to respect our guests' time, be considerate about their money, and reduce their fear, we do still occasionally slip up. And there will always be events that occur outside of our control. The good news is that if we control everything we can and create the most efficient system possible, these interruptions have a much smaller impact. Our system has become so resilient that we can often bounce back quickly. But if something truly major comes up, like several dentists calling in sick or a major storm that makes our employees late or knocks out our power, then we do everything we can to make our customers comfortable. To that end, I've found there are two keys to tempering customer disappointment: transparency and accountability.

As long as people know what to expect and know that you hold yourself to a high standard, they will be understanding. If something you've promised will be late, tell the customer as soon as you know. In our business, if we're behind schedule, our front-of-house staff will update everyone when they check in and tell them how long they can expect to wait. We also make sure to apologize and explain the cause of the delay. If we are facing a major delay, we proactively contact clients to warn them about what to expect and give them a chance to reschedule. Then we hold ourselves accountable and do something to make it up to them. If any of our patients have to wait more than five minutes, our front office staff gives them a Starbucks gift card so they can grab a coffee nearby while they wait. These are relatively small gestures, but they show respect.

MEET CUSTOMERS' CHANGING NEEDS

The battlefield of business is littered with corpses of companies that failed to meet customers' changing needs. Kodak. Blockbuster. PanAm. The countless large brick-and-mortar retailers sunk by Amazon. The list goes on. To stay ahead of changing customer needs, I recommend that you follow the research and development.

STAY CURRENT WITH RESEARCH AND DEVELOPMENT

The computers we all use today feature what's called a graphical user interface (GUI). This interface translates the code within a computer to icons and graphics on the display and allows us to use a mouse and pointer to control the computer. Prior to this (for those readers who, like me, are too young to remember the '70s and early '80s), computer displays mostly consisted of a black screen with green letters and numbers that you controlled with a keyboard. The first commercially viable computer to use this was the Apple Lisa, released in 1983. However, the first computer with a GUI, called the Alto, had been developed a full ten years earlier by an unlikely player: Xerox.

Nowadays, most people think of Xerox as a struggling, more or less defunct photocopier and printer company. At the time, however, Xerox was still a giant. Thirty years before 1983, the first edition of their flagship photocopier had splashed onto the market. They had invested heavily in a novel research and development arm called the Palo Alto Research Center (PARC), which developed, among many other things, laser printing, modems, and, of course, the Alto.

Put simply, Xerox had an opportunity. They had put their resources into the correct methods of inquiry and made breakthroughs that would define the next several decades of computer technology. Instead of trying to push their advantage and invest even deeper into the technology they were developing to find a way to make their computers commercially viable, they took a too early exit ramp. In 1982, Xerox invited Steve Jobs and Steve Wozniak to the PARC to watch an in-depth demo of the Alto computer. In return, Xerox would have the opportunity to buy stock options in Apple in the event they went public.[3]

A quick caveat: It is impossible to know whether or not Xerox could have brought their new computer technology to market. Each individual Alto they produced (more than two thousand, mostly used at the PARC and in universities across the country) cost north of $40,000, which was the equivalent of over $100,000 in 2021. While Xerox had a robust R and D division, manufacturing personal computers obviously represented quite a leap from their core competency of printing and copying.

That being said, they certainly could have tried, and they almost certainly could have gotten more from the technology than they did. They traded away the secret to one of the most important technological innovations in history for the chance to buy stock options in Apple. They didn't seek to develop a partnership that would give them partial ownership over GUIs or anything else like that. And it cost them dearly.

The lesson from all of this is simple: If you invest in R and D and find something that you either know or suspect will make a major difference in the evolution of your industry, follow that research route. Exhaust it. Look for ways to partner with other companies so you can maintain the edge you gleaned from your research and, if you can't do it, gain the benefits of another company that might be better suited to bring that innovation to market.

CHAPTER THREE

Master Your Craft(s)

As a twenty-five-year-old, I almost made one of the worst mistakes an entrepreneur can make: opening a business before I was ready. I had towering confidence and was too naïve to know what I didn't know. Luckily, as I detailed in chapter one, I had enough good sense to pull out of my first office purchase deal, the one where the selling dentist was planning to open a new office in the same area, and instead spent about three years as a dental associate. During that period, I truly mastered my craft and developed the skills that would become the bedrock of Ideal Dental. Every year, hundreds of entrepreneurs make the same mistake I almost made, and many of them end up paying dearly.

Mastering your craft is important because it helps you fill in the details of your grand vision. For example, I knew my grand vision: I wanted to be the Starbucks of dentistry, offering more convenience and better, repeatable results than my competitors. When I started out, I didn't know what that meant in a practical sense. Discovering my customers' desires, as I mentioned, helped me fill in some key details. Working as a dental associate, I saw that they wanted same-day appointments, expanded office hours, all specialties under the same roof, and so on. In addition, and just as important, I deepened my mastery and expertise in dentistry in a way that allowed me to develop innovations that patients didn't even know they wanted. For example, what patient would think to request a 3D scan of their mouth? Most probably know nothing about the scanners (unless they'd had clear braces), or how a 3D image could help them understand their own dental health. I had come across that only because I'd stayed on top of new developments in dental technology and had enough mastery to understand how to find new ways to apply technologies.

It is also vital that you remember that as your business grows, your primary duties change. You'll go from being a practitioner-expert to being a leader. The first half of this chapter addresses industry-specific expertise that you will need to succeed, while the second half addresses how to master leadership.

INDUSTRY-SPECIFIC EXPERTISE

You should know more about your business than anybody else. My personal goal is to learn everything possible about dentistry. This is obviously impossible, but the mindset reminds me to look for any new knowledge I could leverage into an advantage. A recent example is a study I am reviewing on the effect of saliva pH on overall health and the link to other conditions like diabetes and heart disease. That being said, there are certain areas that require a deep degree of mastery, and others where a more surface level understanding will suffice.

DEEP MASTERY

The area that requires the deepest knowledge is your primary craft. Let's take as an example a chef who wants to open a fine-dining restaurant. The one area where they must have absolute expertise is in how to cook in the restaurant's declared style and all the processes that touch that. This expertise will constitute the core pillar of their business. And remember: A master is someone who improves on the previous generation's accomplishments.

Mastery requires innovation. The best sushi chefs don't just slice fish the way they learned from their forebearers. They develop new spice combinations to cure their fish, their own sushi rice recipe, they mix their own sauces and pair it with razor-thin-sliced peppers. They learn to make fresh wasabi by hand in a mixture unique to each chef. They build elaborate eighteen-course tasting menus, giving careful thought to the order in which each piece of fish is served. The more avant-garde ones might invent new techniques to make the bases of sushi, replacing traditional rice with, for example, a green tea cellulose roll.

Likewise, someone running a boutique consulting firm should identify and trade on the expertise they have that makes them unique. Maybe they have a background in business and nuclear physics that makes them particularly attractive for customers in the energy sector. Maybe they spent decades as a Buddhist monk and are extraordinarily adept at training companies to remain calm and present in the face of disaster.

For me, my mastery of dentistry became a core pillar of our company, in addition to everything mentioned in the last chapter. I learned how to numb a patient's gums without them feeling it at all and how to complete each procedure as fast as possible. But most of all, I developed a unique way of building rapport with patients and giving them my full focus no matter the circumstances. I invested time in walking guests through their treatment options and helping them make the best decisions. When I stopped practicing dentistry to work on the business, we modeled our training documents on my processes. I wanted to make sure that even as we expanded, we maintained the quality of care that differentiated us.

The lesson here is that before you know what business to start, you need to figure out where your expertise lies. In other words, don't rush. A lot of the scandals that ended up splashed across business pages—Theranos, FTX, etc.—can be traced back to a founder who let their ambition outstrip their expertise. The best way to create a stable, successful, and scalable business is to provide something customers need and want that nobody else has. And the only way to do that is through deep mastery.

BROAD KNOWLEDGE

"Trust, but verify" is a Russian proverb. It was used often by Ronald Reagan in the context of nuclear disarmament during the Cold War era. You have to have enough basic working knowledge of every aspect of your business to ensure that it is being executed correctly and, if something fails, to know exactly where and how to address the issue. You should know enough about each major part of your company to know where you are and where you want to go. In other words, you need to be able to tell the difference between good and bad performance. Then you can hire a team to get you from where you are to where you want to be.

To return to the dining example, a chef trained at the finest culinary institute who then spends years at home developing the most exquisite recipes would still find plenty of struggle opening a restaurant. The actual recipes represent a mere sliver of the job. As anyone who has read Anthony Bourdain's seminal essay "Hell's Kitchen" knows, a head chef is part cook, part field general, part supply chain manager, and part negotiator.[1]

The head chef develops a menu and daily specials, seeks out the highest-quality ingredients, negotiates with vendors, and follows up when the day's shipment of wild hare shows up twenty minutes late. They prep the food. Manage the entire back- and front-of-house staffs; drill the specials into the waiters; make sure the butchers arrive on time and properly prep the meat; keep the sous-chef, grill master, and salad person all on schedule so the greens don't wilt under a heating lamp while the plate waits for a steak. On top of this, they have to cook themselves, often filling the most complicated orders. And they need to know enough about each of these crafts to hire people who do an exemplary job.

To figure out which secondary skills to master that you plan to delegate, map your entire process from creating or designing your product or service to customer use, and then the post-customer experience. Then find out what high performance and low performance looks like for each skill. Meet with potential vendors, read books about supply chains, keep up to date on research about different materials. This will paint a picture of what competency looks like so when you hire and train people, you know exactly what you're looking for. And you can give your employees concrete goals, hold them accountable, and ultimately, if necessary, tweak your processes or even let people go to ensure top performance.

When I made my own map as a dental associate, the processes I realized I needed to understand were scheduling, cleanings and checkups, dental care, post-treatment process, and billing and insurance. (I'm leaving functions universal to all business, such as advertising and accounting, out because we will address those in later chapters.) Much of what I learned, I learned through observation—I saw the difference between high and low performance in action.

Take, for example, our scheduling software. I don't need to know how to use it or how to install it or necessarily the specs that differentiate options on the market. All I need to know is, does our system work? Does everyone in the office have the information they need when they need it? Is the software intuitive for our front office staff to use or not? Do we often (or ever) accidentally double book time slots? Do people regularly miss their appointments in part because our software doesn't send them enough automated reminder text messages or calls?

Likewise, I could see what made the difference between a good dental assistant or hygienist and a bad one. Some of them had an excellent bedside manner and helped put children at ease during their cleanings and X-rays. Some seemed to rush their work, and I might find traces of plaque build-up on the teeth, or a child obviously frightened in the chair. In terms of post-treatment, I learned that the industry standard was generally to ignore any sort of follow-up with patients, which I found unacceptable.

The big thing I had to go out of my way to learn was billing—most offices' personnel keep dentists insulated from this task. But I knew that I wanted to start a company, so I sought out the financial office. I got an understanding of how long it took most of the major insurers to reimburse, and what the staff did when they had to follow up with a claim, or how they negotiated with an insurance company that tried to avoid paying or wanted to reimburse below normal levels.

EMOTIONAL INTELLIGENCE

Every great business had, at some point, at least one uniquely inspirational leader. I think this might be the most underdiscussed aspect of business success. I see it all the time in the MBA graduates we hire from top business schools. They think in terms of profit and loss, sales and production cycles, and supply chains. Their brains are filled up with extremely complicated (and intelligent) methods they can use to analyze a problem. It's all great. But one thing they never learn in school is how to deal with people. They don't understand that the most successful leaders have figured out how to pair analytic intelligence with emotional intelligence and use that cocktail to inspire people and influence behavior.

Emotional intelligence is a skill that is essential for an entrepreneurial leader. It is cultivated over years, often from an early age, and encompasses how to read and understand people to be relatable and to influence behavior. Among mediocre leaders, this is the one critical skill I have often found lacking. How often have you walked into a room full of people and been able to very quickly size up your audience and adjust yourself to interact accordingly? This skill sets apart the great from the average. I often remind our staff and clinicians that most patients cannot tell the difference between good and average dentistry, but they will always remember how you made them feel. Did you treat them with respect, look them in the eye, address their concern in a manner they understood, and do so confidently? The magic happens even before the actual dental appointment, from the time the phone is answered to schedule an appointment to the time the patient is walked out in a timely manner without feeling any pain. In fact, our front office is trained to answer the phone by asking, "Ideal Dental, how can I make you smile today?" This applies to all businesses. Emotional intelligence is a skill that should be continually developed until it becomes natural.

Doing so requires a whole suite of so-called soft skills, namely the ability to communicate in a way that makes people feel valued. Many managers never figure this out. Instead, they merely communicate by using numbers as both a stick and a carrot (If you don't hit these numbers, you'll be on probation! Only three more sales until you get your bonus!). While goals and standards matter, so does the way they're communicated. If you just use metrics to apply constant pressure, then it can sow dysfunction and unproductive competition among the ranks.

In the worst scenarios, managers sneer at the idea that people skills matter. They fret that empathy and connecting with employees will make them appear weak and impact their ability to demand high performance. These people tend to dismiss emotional intelligence as a desperate need to be liked. But this is a false pretense. A leader obsessed with making sure everyone likes them is just as ineffective as a leader who belittles their employees because they won't hold their employees accountable. Balance is essential. I aim to be compassionate, understanding, and trusting, while still holding myself, my team, and my company to a high standard. Sometimes, effective leadership requires uncomfortable conversations and pushing people to achieve what they didn't believe was possible. Sometimes, although rarely, it even requires outright confrontation. But even those moments of confrontation become easier and more effective if you've mastered emotional intelligence. I know several hyper-talented people who never managed to break out of their technical silos and move into leadership roles because they never learned how to connect with colleagues.

Perhaps part of why empathy and connection remain underdiscussed is because they are difficult to teach. Unlike finance or supply chain management, it's almost impossible to create a generalized theory of emotional intelligence in the same way it's impossible to create an all-encompassing theory for writing or painting. Emotional intelligence is, at the end of the day, a carefully attuned sense, an aliveness and sensitivity to the world, to the people around us, to the moment. And just as each master chef has their unique style, each excellent leader has developed their own approach to managing, inspiring, and supporting people. That approach will, inevitably, be informed by each leader's personal histories and experiences.

So while I cannot offer a step-by-step process of developing emotional intelligence, I can offer reflections from my experience, examples of how I responded to interpersonal challenges, and my thought process behind the decisions that I've made. And I can offer a few practices that can make you more aware of how you interact with other people, so you can begin the process of refining your own emotional intelligence. This is a skill, just like any other. We can all practice it, learn more about how to see an issue from another person's perspective, and discover which buttons to push to encourage people and help them grow. In my experience, the five most important actions to build emotional intelligence are to cultivate empathy, develop resilience, show that you care, practice honesty, and seek different perspectives.

Cultivate Empathy

I was born to two Pakistani doctors in what was then Harare, Rhodesia, a nation that would eventually become Zimbabwe. I spoke Urdu with my parents, English at school, and Shona, a Bantu language, with my Zimbabwean friends. At the time, the area was still under British rule, and I grew up in a practical facsimile of a London suburb. The architecture was the same, the roads were the same. Tea shops and colorful jacaranda trees lined the thruways. There were, however, three major differences between my home and the London suburbs. First, better weather—we actually saw the sun. Second, each day a long string of native Zimbabwean street vendors pushed their carts past our front door. And third, we often experienced rolling citywide blackouts that cut private power, so everyone in the area had to rely on the streetlamps to see or study. Even on days without blackouts I would see kids who didn't have access to a house with electricity gathered under streetlamps to study.

It was there, among the Pakistani and British émigrés and the Zimbabweans, that I first started to cultivate my sense of empathy. A beautiful feature of Zimbabwean culture is an emphasis on community. Everyone cared for and about each other, and life moved at a slower pace to accommodate this ethos. In Zimbabwe, people would sit in the street to chat idly with whatever vendors went past. Almost every transaction was bracketed by, at minimum, pleasantries, if not a full conversation. I couldn't walk down the street without being flagged down by a neighbor for a chat or bumping into a friend. This all put me in the habit of slowing down and asking questions. And since I interacted regularly with such a wide range of people, I began to learn how to seek to understand people's diverse experiences and opinions at a very young age. I continue this habit even now, and when I find myself feeling busy or rushed, I remind myself to slow down. I stay present with whomever I'm talking to, ask as many questions as I can, and take time to process new ideas as I encounter them.

As I got older, I went through two jarring experiences, both of which deepened my ability to empathize, albeit in different ways. First, as a child I'd lived through the revolution that ended British colonial rule and brought Robert Mugabe to power, where he would remain for my entire childhood and beyond. This brought a great deal of hardship to my community, and in response, I had to learn to empathize with others as they struggled in this new world. Suddenly, I was in an impoverished segment of an impoverished and war-torn country. Some of my closest friends recounted to me stories of hiding beneath the bed when they were twelve or thirteen years of age while soldiers executed their parents. One of my parents' good friends, a man who used to come by to help them around the house, died of complications related to AIDS in the 1980s. This was the reality I grew up in, learning about the hardships that other people faced, witnessing the losses my friends suffered and the sacrifices my parents made while contending with hardship myself.

Then, after all that, I came to the United States and experienced intense culture shock. I flew for about twenty hours from Zimbabwe to Detroit. After going through customs, I had a layover before my final flight down to Jacksonville, where I would start college. I was starving, exhausted, and more than a bit anxious. I went to a Burger King, and the woman behind the counter said, with a curtness that would be taboo in Zimbabwe, "What do you want?"

No "Hi, how are you today? How was your flight?"

I was taken aback, and mumbled something like, "A Whopper and chips." She couldn't understand me, so I repeated it, a bit more loudly, "A Whopper with chips."

She said, "We don't have chips."

I was shocked. The menu was plastered with pictures of chips.

"Yes you do," I said. "They're all over the menu."

"Those are fries," she snappily said.

Finally, I got my order in. This was my first hint that America would be unlike anything I'd experienced. In Zimbabwe, nobody ever rushed. People there harbored ambitions, sure, but they seldom let them dominate their lives.

In America, however, everyone seemed to sprint from activity to activity. It seemed that the rush came from the desire, the need, to consume. More food, more clothes, the latest AirPods and iPhones and hoverboards and augmented reality goggles, new cars, another house, whatever. The drive to consume, the capacity to want, is dramatically higher in the United States than what I'd grown up with. This difference probably owes something to the level of opportunity available. In America, it's possible to advance in life to a degree that would be simply unheard of in Zimbabwe. I felt a tremendous sense of possibility, and I adapted by making it my goal to seize these new opportunities.

But just because I embraced bigger goals didn't mean I let go of the mindset I had picked up in Zimbabwe. Nor did it mean I forgot about what I'd lived through, about my intimate knowledge with how we all face crisis and challenge and suffering in life. I integrated this mindset into who I was, but I hold it lightly. When I talk to anyone, I strive to understand their values, how they see the world, their challenges and how I can help them carry a burden. I do my best to always remember that everyone, regardless of their background, has a unique story and valuable knowledge to share.

Develop Resilience

We usually think of resilience—the ability to navigate and overcome setbacks—as the grit that people need to succeed. While that is true, resilience is also an underappreciated aspect of emotional intelligence. Simply put, it's easy to be empathetic and caring when everything is going well for you, whereas people are much more likely to lash out in stressful times. True resilience isn't just the ability to overcome challenges but the ability to face those challenges calmly, to stay in the moment, to communicate productively, and to rally colleagues. Since striving to achieve a grand vision often keeps one in a near-constant state of fear, resilience is one of the most important traits to develop.

I owe my resilience to my upbringing and experience as an immigrant. My parents, as doctors, led busy lives. From a young age if I wanted to do anything, I had to make it happen myself. For example, as a teenager, I became obsessed with squash. The closest place to practice was about one mile from my house. Every day I would come home from school while my parents were still working. I would drop off my bags, bike to the squash courts, and play for as long as possible before biking home in the dark.

When I was thirteen, I had a chance to compete in the national under-fourteen squash championships. The tournament was several miles away, and, as usual, I had to take myself there by bike. I'd held onto a thin hope that my family would come to watch. But although hundreds of people showed up to watch the tournament, I played alone. I made it to the finals, where I ended up going down two sets to zero. The match was a best of five sets, and I felt my situation was hopeless. I distinctly remember looking at the hundreds of spectators, and though I didn't see my family, I did not feel deflated.

Before the third set, I sat on the bench and took some deep breathes. I put the previous two sets to the side, and I told myself to focus on the next point. If I won that point, I could win the one after that, and so on. Play resumed, and I won the next point. And then the next one. And another. Eventually, I'd picked up the set.

After, I didn't even look into the crowd. My whole world existed in those four walls. I wasn't worried about the score or my family or anything. I was in the moment, reacting seamlessly to the ball as it came off the wall. The fourth set started like the third, with me streaming out to a large early lead. Eventually, I took the set.

And the fifth, I barely remember. It was a blur of motion, thumping heart, sweat. I was in the zone. Suddenly, it was over. I'd won.

I jumped and cheered, and as I walked off the court, jubilant, a man's hand landed on my shoulder. I looked up, and it was my father. He was smiling and told me how proud he was and how sorry he was to have missed the earlier matches.

I could have collapsed under the pressure, under my opponent's stellar early play, under the disappointment of playing without a loved one in the stands. But I didn't. Instead, I used the desperation of the situation to keep myself present. I broke everything down and took it one moment at a time. By the time I looked up from the details, I'd already won.

As an immigrant, I had to find new reservoirs of resilience. I came to America alone, not because my family couldn't afford to come, but because I wanted to learn how to navigate my new home on my own. It was a baptism by fire approach, and baptized I was! On my first day in the States, after I had finally managed to get my Whopper and fries, my flight from Detroit to Florida was delayed. This was before cell phones, so I couldn't coordinate with the representative from my school's international students' office who was supposed to pick me up. I landed in Jacksonville well after midnight and found nobody waiting for me. I took a $40 cab to the university, and when the cab driver asked what building I was going to, I told him I didn't know.

He took me to the only building still open: the campus police station. Since I didn't know what my dorm was, the police couldn't do much to help me. I spent the night on a bench in the station under harsh fluorescent lights with the sound of radios and jiggles of handcuffs echoing around me. In the morning, I finally connected with my rep from the international students' office; he took me to my dorm room, and then left. That was about all the support I got. I discovered that the dorm room was empty—no sheets, no pillows, just a bed and desk. I balled up some T-shirts to make a pillow and used a towel as a sheet.

The next day, I discovered that in America you need a car to get around. I didn't even have my license in Zimbabwe, much less an international license. I couldn't drive to get supplies or food. It was before Uber, so for the first month I ate at the on-campus Pizza Hut and Subway.

This was shaping into one of the worst stretches of my life.

I'd ended up in Jacksonville because when I was applying to schools, everything I knew about the US came from the TV show *Baywatch*. I wanted to live like the characters on the show: a life of sun, waves, sand, and beautiful people jogging in slow motion. I went to the US consulate in Harare and asked where they shot *Baywatch*. The woman behind the counter told me Florida. The consulate had a copy of the Barron's college guide, and I turned to the Florida page. After reading the materials available, I decided to apply to two schools, the University of Miami and the University of North Florida in Jacksonville. I knew very little about college rankings and hardly knew where the different states were geographically located. Next, I learned I had to take an SAT test to apply to these two schools. The next available one was in two weeks. I showed up completely unprepared. When the instructor told us to "bubble in your responses," I was beyond confused. I had never done nor heard of a multiple-choice test before this.

Then in July 1997, one month before my departure for the States, Gianni Versace was murdered in Miami. That was the only piece of news from Florida that made it to Zimbabwe that year. My dad saw the coverage one Sunday morning on CNN and decided I could not go to Miami. My parents were panicked. They thought if Versace, a rich man with all sorts of protection, could get murdered in Miami, it must be a far too dangerous place for someone like me.

But my heart was set on the *Baywatch* beaches, so I argued with my parents until we reached a compromise. I would attend the University of North Florida, in Jacksonville. During my first week in Jacksonville, I told a new friend that I'd chosen Jacksonville because I wanted to live where they shot *Baywatch*. He laughed and told me that they shot *Baywatch* in California. This was my start in the land of opportunity: I was completely clueless and lost.

I was so miserable, I almost quit. The phones in our dorms couldn't dial internationally, so to talk to my parents I needed to use a pay phone. To do that, I needed a phone card. Luckily, the campus bookstore sold them. I bought one, scratched off the covering to reveal the PIN and dialed my family's number. My father picked up, and near tears I asked if I could come home. He sympathized with me and told me he wouldn't judge me if I came home, but he made me promise that I would stay for at least three more weeks. And then he said something that might be one of the most important lessons I've ever received: "Think about it as a vacation. You are already all the way out there—enjoy yourself, relax. Go to class or don't. Do whatever you want. And if after three weeks you want to come home, then come home."

I promised him I would, and when I hung up the phone, I instantly felt much better. I knew that in three short weeks, I would be at home where I was comfortable. Suddenly, I no longer faced a never-ending stretch of discomfort and dislocation. It was finite. And as humans, we can survive almost anything so long as we know when it will end.

Because I no longer worried about how I'd fit in or felt the need to strategize for the future, I didn't feel as much social pressure as I had before. I focused on fun. I went to a lot of parties. I read the books I wanted to and went to the beach. I slept in a bit and even dropped by a couple of classes. My natural ability to listen, ask questions, and joke around kicked in. In no time at all, I had a tight-knit group of friends. One of them drove me to a store so I could buy linens and towels.

Before the three weeks were up, I called my dad and told him I was going to stay. By the time I finished my first year, I was almost feeling too comfortable. Jacksonville, while lovely, felt a bit small. I wanted a more diverse and dynamic experience, so I researched schools to transfer to. The University of Texas at Dallas seemed ideal, and I finished my undergraduate degree there.

Now when I face other moments of incredible stress, I think about the conversation I had with my dad. It would be going way too far to say I try to reframe business disruptions as vacations. But I do reframe them as exciting challenges, ones that offer chances to develop new ideas, to surprise myself with my capabilities. Today when I feel stressed, I remind myself that everything is temporary and what feels like the end of the world one moment might lose almost all its significance in a couple of weeks. In other words, stay present. Find people who will support you through the dark moments, and you will see the brightness of a new day.

Show You Care

In those early years, I described Ideal Dental as a rocket ship we built while we flew it. We were going so fast and working so hard that we didn't have time to run hundreds of calculations and perfectly plan everything we did. It felt risky and invigorating. I was asking people to work harder than they ever had in their lives, to take risks, and to go on a tremendous journey with me. And they did, but only because I'd earned their trust. They believed we would finish the rocket ship in time to launch it through the atmosphere without ending up in pieces in the Gulf of Mexico. The backbone of that trust wasn't my technical ability or business acumen, but rather the fact that each employee knew I cared about them as much as I cared about the business. It wasn't just that I empathized with their positions, but I actually let that empathy inspire action that helped them. They felt valued and supported and were willing to pour all their brilliance and energy into my grand vision.

Competitive compensation and benefits, opportunities for advancement, and placing a high premium on workplace respect constitute the bare minimum a leader can do to show they care about their teams. From there, I recommend going above and beyond to show compassion for each employee. I made this a habit, and there are several examples that stand out.

First, one of our employees got pregnant. The insurance we provide usually covers four weeks of paid maternity leave, but because she had a specific preexisting condition, the insurance only covered two weeks for her. She was distraught. She couldn't imagine recovering enough from giving birth in two weeks to return to work, not to mention the stress she felt at the idea of entrusting a two-week-old newborn to a caretaker. She considered quitting or trying to negotiate some unpaid time off. As soon as I heard about her dilemma, I called her into my office and told her that the company would guarantee her the full four weeks of paid maternity leave, plus an additional four weeks leave out of our pocket. We then made it company policy to guarantee four weeks of paid maternity leave to every employee, regardless of insurance, so no employee ever had to face the same dilemma again.

Another example comes from an earlier time in our company. We had a young man, twenty-four years old, working in our insurance claims department. One night, he went to sleep and didn't wake up. It was a completely unexpected tragedy. When I heard, I asked when the funeral was so I could pay my respects. I heard the family wasn't sure if they'd be able to pay for the funeral. Much of his family had been relying on his income, so they truly had no funds for services. I assured the young man's family that I would cover the cost of the funeral so everyone would have a chance to come together, grieve, and process their emotions.

Then there was an older woman working for us whose daughter had tragically died. She had stepped up to raise her grandchildren, which was part of why she spent her golden years working for Ideal Dental. When she told me about her situation, I gave her and the grandchildren an all-expenses paid trip to Disney World as a gift. Another elderly woman who worked in our revenue cycle department got cancer and had to leave the company. She lived alone, so for the next three months, I had meals delivered to her house every single day until she moved closer to family. She survived the cancer, thankfully, but retired after that.

I hate sharing these sorts of stories because I want to honor the privacy of the moments I shared with these people. But I believe they impart a powerful and underdiscussed lesson about how to create a caring, service-oriented culture. As a result, everyone feels buoyed by our organization, they trust one another, and they trust their leaders. And we all work as a cohesive unit because of it.

Practice Honesty

The ability to communicate honestly without judgment and without insulting the listener is a pillar of emotional intelligence. This is especially important for a leader who needs to hold people accountable. Failure in this area causes huge problems. In my experience, people make one of two major mistakes in this regard. The most common is that they fear confrontation. They don't want to hurt anyone's feelings, and therefore avoid raising the issue. Truth is, most people want to know how they're doing, especially if they're not doing well. It's better to know where you stand and to have an idea of how to improve than to be moving forward with the illusion you're performing up to par when you're not.

For example, in 2022 a member of my executive team complained to me about one of his direct reports. He claimed that this woman, who was responsible for recruiting new employees, wasn't hitting her numbers, and he wanted to let her go. I knew the employee in question, and asked if he had communicated to her where she was falling short. He said yes, so I told him to give her a chance to correct course. A few weeks later, he came back, saying nothing had changed, so I asked if I could sit in the next meeting between the two of them. At that meeting, I asked her to evaluate her own performance. She answered, "I think I've been doing great."

Clearly, the executive had misled both me and the employee. I said, "Well, I don't think that's the case. If you look at the numbers, you're falling short in these categories."

I went through the numbers with her, and she thanked me. She said she had no idea she wasn't doing well and was glad to know what to aim for. I filed this meeting away as a potential problem.

I asked if she needed any support, and she said yes, that she wanted to talk to someone in a different department about a new initiative she wanted to implement to attract new recruits. I loved the idea and made the connection.

Before the meeting, the inaccurate info had obscured the actual problem, and therefore the possible solutions. Our honest conversations led to real, quick change. I also filed this moment away for future reference. I figured that either the executive had never actually told the employee about her performance and lied to me that he had, or that he had tried to communicate the problems the employee had but could not do so in a clear enough way. Either way could lead to more problems down the road, so I asked the executive to work on communicating more clearly.

Another common mistake is to unload abuse under the guise of honesty. From what I've observed, this approach arises from a mistaken belief that employees will only perform if they feel pressure and fear. As a result, some managers use threats or claim their subordinate's underperformance is indicative of some personal failing, saying, for example, "If you actually cared about your job, you wouldn't be failing." But these statements are no more honest than telling someone they're doing great when they aren't. They're hyperboles that reflect more about the emotional state and fear of the speaker than about the employee's performance. And because it's hyperbolic, it's counterproductive. Not only does this type of communication damage an employee's self-esteem, but it also leaves them bereft of inspiration to improve their performance.

In my experience, providing employees with clear performance metrics serves as a powerful tool to increase productivity without the need for personal attacks. Numbers are objective. When you reference them in a conversation, instead of making what you say a critique based on interpretation or about some aspect of their personality, you can tie any objection to the metrics. This is how I handled the conversation with the employee in the example above, and she was able to receive the feedback without taking it as a judgment of her worth or as a blow to her self-esteem. To the contrary, she left the meeting feeling more motivated than before.

Seek Different Perspectives

As a leader, a sizeable part of your job becomes helping employees navigate interpersonal conflicts and, at times, serving as an arbitrator to maintain a healthy, productive work environment. This really is the core of emotional intelligence and why it matters. To do this effectively, you need to seek as many perspectives as possible before making any decisions or brokering new agreements.

Let's return to the above example with the new executive and his direct report. A bit after the three of us met, I asked the executive for an update to see if the other employee had made progress. He told me he still thought we should let her go. According to him, her performance was still lagging, and she got too emotional whenever he tried to encourage her to do better.

The facts didn't seem to tie together for me. In the meeting with the three of us, she hadn't become emotional at all. She took the feedback with grace and resilience, and even seemed thankful for the concrete steps forward.

This time, instead of taking the executive at his word, I decided to hear her view on the situation. I called her and asked for an update. She told me she was doing well and gave me some data to support that her projects were on the right track. She then thanked me again for the feedback earlier, and she also mentioned that she couldn't stand her supervisor, the executive.

I asked why, and she said, "Well, after the three of us spoke, he called me into his office and told me that I was a terrible leader, that nobody took me seriously, and that's why I haven't been able to do my job. I started to cry, and he said, 'See, that's exactly what I mean. You're crying. That's a sign of weakness, and it's why people don't respect you.'"

I believed her. I'd known her for years and had never known her to behave in the way the executive described. It seemed clear that her supervisor had used the guise of being honest to dole out abuse.

He seemed to know he'd made a mistake and tried to cover his rear by discrediting her. This infuriated me. He hadn't merely lied, but also had reached for ugly misogynistic stereotypes about women (They're irrational! They're too emotional! They're not strong enough!) in an attempt to obscure his mistake. Our company happens to employ 80 percent women, and I couldn't have someone with such obvious biases in a position of power.

But before I acted, I wanted more information. As I always say: trust, but verify. I thanked her for her honesty and told her I wanted to contact his other direct reports to better understand his management style. I asked who she thought I should talk to, while reassuring her that I wouldn't mention her or our conversation to anyone. She gave me three names, and I called them first.

What I heard from those three was so jarring that I called every single one of his direct reports. I ended up with a litany of complaints, and a portrait of a leader with extremely limited emotional intelligence. He would text people constantly, either first thing in the morning, well before 9:00 AM, or as late as 10:30 PM. He had no respect for people who were married or had kids, and he would even call on the weekends. If they complained, he would go on some rant about how he was their boss, and they needed to answer whenever he called or get back to him within an hour even on weekends. He would often belittle his employees.

Don't get me wrong—I believe in hard work. I work weekends. I've made countless sacrifices to build my business to the level we have reached. But I recognize that I'm willing to do that because it's my baby. As nice as it would be for everyone to show the same degree of commitment, that will never happen. And even I've always made sure to spend time with my family, even during the most stressful times in my business.

When I finished my interviews, I let this executive go as soon as I could. I usually prefer to give people a chance to change their behavior and improve their performance, but in this situation I knew I had to move quickly. He had already damaged the ecosystem of trust and respect that we had worked hard to cultivate. Additionally, he'd proven he would lie to cover up his actions rather than take responsibility. The scary thing is that if I hadn't interviewed the employees, I would have never known about this. Like a real Jekyll and Hyde, he knew how to manage up—presenting a face to me and the board that everything was going well, that he was an amicable, levelheaded manager, before turning around and subjecting his reports to terrible behavior.

This is what leadership and emotional intelligence is all about. I protected my people and created an environment where they would feel comfortable and have the tools to succeed. I asked careful questions to understand the source and nature of the problem. I feel great pride that my employees felt comfortable being honest with me about their experience with this executive. It showed that I'd earned their trust, that they knew I cared about them and wouldn't side with someone merely because of their position on the organizational chart. Thankfully, I was able to cut this cancer out before it could metastasize.

MASTERY IS A PROCESS, NOT A DESTINATION

The closer you are to mastery, the more you understand it's impossible to achieve. Perfection doesn't exist. There's always more to learn, and your situation always changes. In business, the best path to growth is to continue to deepen your mastery and continue to let that mastery lead to more innovation. The minute you stop innovating is the minute your business starts to die. You can find the headstones of many once-great businesses in the graveyard

> ***The closer you are to mastery, the more you understand it's impossible to achieve. Perfection doesn't exist.***

of great innovators who got too comfortable and stopped innovating. Kodak, Blockbuster, Nokia, Yahoo, Xerox, MySpace, Atari—the list could fill pages.

From 2008 to 2023, Ideal Dental has had to innovate through several shifts in business and dentistry. During that time, digital marketing became the most dominant advertising strategy, bolstered by the widespread adoption of smartphones. New dental technologies emerged, and we had to adopt to stay on top. While I don't follow each dental innovation with the same fervor I did early on, I do have a chief medical officer who oversees a clinical board of about thirty-five dentists. His only job is to track the most recent innovations in dentistry. I talk to my chief medical officer consistently. He's my right-hand man. When he finds an innovation he likes, he runs it by me, and we do a pilot study in one of our offices. If it works, we adopt it in all of our offices.

Our clinical practice is the core of our company. If we ever slip up in the quality of care that we offer or lose our leading edge, the costs would devastate our business. For that reason, we keep moving forward and invest to deepen our mastery so we can remain the cutting-edge leaders. Every time we have reached a new level of understanding, we've realized how much more there is to learn. This feeling is both discouraging and beautiful. It speaks to the extreme trials and joys of life, and shows we can always be surprised and challenged and always improve. We can grow and evolve infinitely, always uncovering a more complete and more competent version of ourselves.

CHAPTER

FOUR

Brand It

The internationally renowned artist Andy Warhol once said,

> You can be watching TV and see Coca-Cola, and you know that the president drinks Coke, Liz Taylor drinks Coke, and just think, you can drink Coke, too. A Coke is a Coke and no amount of money can get you a better Coke than the one the bum on the corner is drinking. All the Cokes are the same and all the Cokes are good. Liz Taylor knows it, the president knows it, the bum knows it, and you know it.

This perfectly articulates the power of branding. A great brand is recognizable. It is desirable. It makes people feel happy and safe. And it delivers a consistent, predictable experience. Nobody buys a Coke and frets about botulism. And as a brand becomes more well-known, it starts to shine like gold. I mean that somewhat literally. Investors tend to give brands a much higher valuation than no-name entities because of the trust that brands inspire. That sheen also aids recruiting. In the same way that Harvard and Stanford attract the most accomplished applicants, the brands with the best reputations attract the best talent.

WHAT BRANDING ISN'T

First of all, I want to bust what I view as the biggest (and most costly) myth about branding: the idea that *branding* means creating clever slogans, pleasing images, names, and funny TV ads. Those are merely the most superficial aspects of a brand, the most visible and least important. Most companies funnel huge chunks of cash to PR firms and brand consultants, often with negligible impact on public perception.

For example, in 2021, Uber spent $1.7 billion on advertising.[1] That same year, the product review blog RaveReviews used an algorithm designed by a computer science professor from the University of Wolverhampton to analyze millions of tweets and determine which brand was the most hated, at least on Twitter (now X). The winner? Uber! With merely 50 percent of the tweets about the company being negative, their large ad spend clearly wasn't enough to overcome the issues that led to their most-hated status, specifically driver compensation, rider safety, and surge pricing.[2]

Obviously, this doesn't mean that 50 percent of people in the world hate Uber. The study covered a small sample that was skewed toward Twitter users who felt passionately enough to tweet about a company. But the study provides a data point that indicates you can't spend your way to a positive brand image. Consumers form their opinions about a company based on their personal experiences and those they hear about from people they know, not based on slogans or TV spots.

The core of your brand must come down to what your company presents, how it meets your customers' needs, and how well you solve customers' concerns around time, money, and fear. In the coming chapters I will talk about creating processes to ensure you deliver an exceptional experience, but for now I will talk about one of the more intangible ingredients for excellence: culture.

YOUR CULTURE IS YOUR BRAND

It might seem at first that culture is a purely internal aspect of your business, but it is my aim to convince you that culture is central to your brand. It is the content of your culture that determines which lasting impressions your brand will create.

A company's culture and guiding values determine how the company treats employees and how those employees treat customers. A front office employee who feels disrespected and doesn't like their job is more likely to leave a customer waiting while the employee meanders through a personal call. That one rude, dismissive employee will become the brand's avatar for that customer. Likewise, an engaged, happy, and respected front office employee is more likely to be attentive, efficient, and polite. For that customer, the happy front office person becomes the brand's avatar.

In essence, your culture becomes your brand. So before you pour tens of thousands of dollars into marketing and advertising, make sure you've got a solid foundation for a healthy culture in place.

CULTIVATING THE RIGHT CULTURE FOR YOUR BRAND

What does a healthy culture look like to you? What sort of culture do you want to cultivate? This is the thorniest question when creating a brand, made pricklier due to the mercurial nature of a company culture.

Culture is a broad term we use to describe how each worker's individual personality, values, and actions interact with the business's structure, actions, mission, rules, and standards. Each of those variables changes frequently, if not constantly. On top of that, no matter how great your systems are, each department and location will develop their own subculture that can change from day to day.

At Ideal Dental, we strive toward what I call a service culture. The core idea of a service culture is that we are not in the dental business serving people, we are in the people business serving dentistry. In other words, our first concern is the people. Another of my favorite mantras is that we are people taking care of people. If we take care of each other, a quality guest experience will follow naturally.

The giving-back culture has served us well, but it's ultimately up to you to decide how you want to define the culture you want. Whatever you choose, the actions I list below will contribute to a productive and healthy workplace environment. They are: take it personally, set your core values, hire the right people, prioritize service, adapt to challenges, practice transparency, and work hard to play hard.

Take It Personally

If you care enough about something, it becomes personal. Some founders and owners hide behind their brands in an attempt to dodge responsibility for their company's actions. I recommend that you do the opposite. I am my brand. I consider every negative review a direct reflection of me. I have a deep conviction that my company can and will provide the best service imaginable, and I won't tolerate anything that undermines that belief. I recommend every founder do the same. My rabid devotion to my brand motivates me to work harder than anyone else, step in to do any job, and strive to undo

> ***If you care enough about something, it becomes personal.***

any negative perception of Ideal Dental. That dedication radiates throughout the company. When my team sees how much I care and how much pride I take in my work, they're inspired to do the same.

Without this degree of belief, a brand suffers. Take, for example, McDonald's, purchased decades ago by Ray Kroc, who also served as the company's CEO. They rose to prominence by offering cheap, tasty burgers in a clean, family-friendly environment. According to business expert Daniel Coyle's bestselling book, *The Culture Code*, Kroc set a high standard for McDonald's. He was famous for cleaning any McDonald's location he walked into.[3] He picked up every cup and wrapper that a customer left on the tables, floor, or even strewn across the parking lot or garden. In one story, he used an old toothbrush to scrub gunk out of the holes in the mop wringer. He clearly took his brand personally, and his dedication set the tone.

In 1984, Kroc died. In the 1990s and early 2000s, McDonald's became synonymous with dingy digs, déclassé décor, and dirt. They even installed intentionally uncomfortable seating to encourage patrons to eat fast and get out.[4] In the 2010s, as a response to the cleaner and healthier fast-casual chains such as Panera Bread and Chipotle eating into their market share, McDonald's rebooted. They made their interiors sleeker and reprioritized cleanliness. Now their interiors are so nice and comfortable that if it weren't for the menus, you might confuse any McDonald's for a Starbucks. But they never would have had to execute this turnaround if they hadn't let their commitment to quality flag in the first place. The lesson is clear: Dedicate yourself to your brand to the point that it is an extension of yourself. Then set a tone by showing employees how much you care.

For years I attended Ideal Dental grand openings, and in the days leading up to them, I personally helped spick-and-span the new office. On opening day, I would gather the new employees for a discussion, emphasizing why we exist, our goals, and what makes Ideal Dental unique. I would review our core values and remind them that they were embarking on a noble job of healing and service. It's small things like this that show conviction and keep a brand strong as it grows and transforms. While our rate of growth has made it impossible for me to attend each opening (sometimes we have multiple openings on the same day), I still make it a point to go to as many locations as I can and to meet as many of our new employees face-to-face as possible.

Once you've decided to take your brand personally, you need to do the hard work to make sure you deliver predictable and uniform excellence. This challenge only gets greater as you scale because it becomes more difficult to personally connect with your employees and to oversee quality control.

Set Your Core Values

Your core values are how you communicate the type of culture you want to create to your employees. Ideal Dental has five core values:

1. **I**ntegrity: We do what we say we will do.
2. **D**iscipline: We are dedicated to a consistent and repeatable process.
3. **E**xcellence: We always strive to be the best.
4. **A**ccountability: We are responsible for our words, our actions, and our results.
5. **L**oyalty: We are loyal to our guests and to each other.

These five values all pivot around one idea: service. We serve each other first and create an environment where everyone feels welcome. As of 2022, women comprised 80 percent of our workforce and minorities comprised almost 50 percent. We are a truly meritocratic organization. We hire the best person for the job and then create a culture that respects everyone regardless of their gender, race, religion, or sexual identity.

When we come together to serve our guests, we provide the best care possible and have the discipline to do what we must, the integrity to keep our word, the accountability to own our mistakes, and the loyalty to ensure we always put each other above all else. We distribute laminated cards with these values and we have our employees memorize them. We reiterate them in meetings. The point is to remind people how they should act and why it matters that they execute their jobs to the best of their abilities. In my experience, this is a vital step and one that significantly boosts both employees' well-being and overall productivity.

Research shows a well-established link between culture and company success. Charles Duhigg, an internationally recognized expert on habits and productivity, argued in a 2019 article in *The New Yorker* that Amazon's culture, especially among corporate and managerial employees, was an essential part of Amazon's success. According to Duhigg, Amazon reenforced their culture by distributing laminated cards with leadership principles, essentially a mix of maxims and core values. The employees studied these cards as if they were Talmudic texts and worked to follow the dicta whenever possible.

The principles include exhortations for employees to "examine their strongest convictions with humility," not to "compromise for the sake of social cohesion," to commit to excellence, that "frugality breeds resourcefulness, self-sufficiency, and invention," and that speed matters.[5] Everything that made Amazon successful—their aversion to wasteful spending, their commitment to hyperefficient delivery, their dedication to excellence, their ability to adapt and change rapidly—is contained in these principles. According to Duhigg, each corporate and managerial employee completely internalized these principles, which is what allowed Amazon to grow exponentially. Everyone developed new innovations at breakneck speed and in alignment with the company.

We strive to do the same, and it has been a key contributor to our rapid growth. I recommend you do as well.

Hire the Right People

Every employee contributes to culture. Of course, some employees carry more cultural weight than others. In the macro sense, the founder or CEO has the most influence. But on a location-by-location or department-by-department basis, any given employee can shape the culture more than the corporate leaders. For example, at Ideal if we hire a grouchy dentist who yells at the support staff, hardly talks to guests, and works slowly and sloppily, they could easily harm the entire office's culture. Even a receptionist with a negative disposition can create friction and drag an entire office down. This is a big part of why I see hiring as the most important process in a business. Since I consider my brand as an extension of me, each employee who represents that brand is also an extension of me.

We aim to only hire candidates who display our five core values, who will fit in with our culture, and who will work to further our founding mission. A candidate's values are one of our most important criteria. We know that if someone is willing to hold themselves accountable to our values, our standard of excellence, then we will be able to teach them any technical skill they need. It's much more challenging to teach core values.

To that end, we partnered with a company that creates culture profile assessments that we give to all hiring candidates. Together, we developed a customized seven-minute survey that measures traits such as assertiveness, logical reasoning, attention to detail, and emotional intelligence. The company we hired uses this data to develop an archetype or profile that describes what sort of employee the candidate might be. For the most part, especially when we hire for any leadership or customer-facing role, we look for what are called servant leaders. These people usually score low on ego and aggressiveness, and high on empathy, dedication, hard work, and assertiveness—traits that indicate they're willing to hold people accountable, they care less about individual accolades than overall success, and they will be able to empathize with the customers. Of course, we look for different qualities for each position. For example, someone crunching numbers in accounting doesn't need to be particularly assertive or emotionally intelligent. They need to be detail oriented and hardworking.

Myriad companies offer similar services, and I suggest that once you reach about one hundred employees, or once you have to start to rely on other people to make hiring decisions, you find a company to develop a similar survey. I will caution: Don't use these surveys as the only metric. As with any other personality test, candidates can game these by responding in ways that they hope will make them more appealing. At Ideal, we work to build a holistic view of each candidate, of which the survey is merely a part. We also place a great deal of weight on interviews and references. As with almost anything else, effectively interviewing candidates and references are unique skills, and I've found there are some tricks that help get a more accurate sense of the candidate.

For interviews, I always ask questions that correspond to our core values. I might ask, for an example, about a mistake they made and how they handled it, or how they overcame a challenge. Or I may ask them to describe a disagreement they had with a peer and what they did to resolve it. But these are somewhat standard questions, and I usually receive well-rehearsed responses. I'm most curious about what someone says when caught off guard because that tells me more about how they respond and think on the fly.

To that end, I will pepper in a few questions that seem innocuous, that don't have any wrong answers. For example, I might ask, "What do you do for fun?" I then interpret their responses. If someone says something like (and this has actually happened), "Well, on weekends I go and volunteer at a food bank," that tells me a lot. I love service as much as anyone else—I've built my entire company around it. But volunteering still is work. Maybe it's part of what they do for fun, but it's a very calculated and guarded answer. If that person hadn't listed volunteer experience on their résumé, it would throw up even more red flags. In that case, I'd most likely assume they were lying. Regardless, I'd follow up with whatever organization they claim to have volunteered with to make sure.

If, on the other hand, I was interviewing a young person just out of college, and they told me something like, "Well, most Fridays, my friends from college and I go to karaoke night, and I also like to rock climb," that strikes me as more honest. Or if someone were to say, "Well, I'm a single mother, so I don't have a ton of time on my own, and I just cherish the chance to go on adventures with my daughter," that would give me a lot of information about her priorities. It shows that she has a sense of responsibility and cares about supporting the people around her. Of course, the answers to these questions are just another data point for my hiring decisions.

Calling references presents its own challenge. I've found that people listed as references seldom speak honestly about the candidate. Usually, the candidate chooses the people for references because they know they will give glowing reviews, and usually the reference does just that. When I ask a reference about the candidate's weakness, I usually get a tailored answer designed to seem honest while still painting the candidate in an unrealistically positive light. So I flip the question, and ask, "If you could give me one piece of advice to help me help this person succeed, what would it be?" Any answer to this question will be far more honest and give me insight into a prospect's weaknesses.

Instead of asking the reference to slander someone they care about, I'm inviting them to help the candidate. Plus this approach lowers the reference's guard because it makes it sound like I'm close to hiring this person, whether or not that's true. For example, someone might tell me,

"Well, frankly, this person's creative but a bit scatterbrained—you will probably have to micromanage them until they internalize your processes enough that they become second nature." Or I might hear something like, "This person is a charismatic leader, but they sometimes struggle to hold people accountable, so you might want to create a system that allows their supervisor to make sure every project stays on track." Not only does this tell me (or whoever in my company is doing the hiring) way more about the prospect's habits, it also gives us a hint of how to help our new hires succeed.

Sometimes, in spite of our best efforts, someone who doesn't align with our culture slips through the cracks. Usually we find out pretty quickly, and we move on quickly to give that person a chance to find a situation better suited to their strengths. The executive I spoke about at length in chapter 3 is an example of this. We obviously thought he would be an excellent fit in our culture based on the interviews, but we were wrong.

To prevent a similar situation from recurring, I added a new step to the hiring process for high-level leaders. Instead of just calling the references they list on their applications, we also call their direct reports. We ask them questions about the leader's emotional intelligence, demeanor, and ability to handle pressure, inspire, and coach. Respect matters to our company culture. I don't want someone who just knows how to put on a good show for the board and C-suite. I want someone who lives our values and who treats the people they manage with dignity.

Of course, the best way to avoid bringing in someone whose values don't match yours is not to bring in new people at all. We always try to promote from within whenever possible. That way we know for a fact the employee is committed to upholding our culture. Sometimes, however, that's not feasible, especially when it comes to executive-level hires.

Prioritize Service

It's not enough to talk about a commitment to service, you also need to act on that commitment. Perhaps the most famous example of an unparalleled service culture is the Ritz-Carlton, and in the early days I borrowed as much as I could from them. The Ritz-Carlton understands the importance of investing in employees, so they mandate that each employee spend at least 250 hours a year in paid training programs. They also have developed a robust system for employees to share feedback—both positive and negative—about their experiences. They have an internal forum where anyone can post either commendations or complaints. Managers monitor this discussion board and react accordingly. They regularly conduct employee engagement surveys and take action if they notice engagement waning. This is all with the goal of retaining their workers because they believe that great service comes from establishing relationships. They want the employees to get to know frequent travelers and repeat guests, so when they arrive, they're recognized immediately by the employees and greeted by name. So to maximize retention, the Ritz-Carlton pays attention to and takes care of their employees. In many ways, that's how a service culture starts: with a company serving their own employees and inspiring the employees to pay that dedication forward.

Because the Ritz-Carlton invests so much in training programs, they feel they can trust their employees. To that end, almost every single Ritz-Carlton employee has a budgeted amount of discretionary spending—company money they can use to satisfy a customer need, whether that's comping a dinner that took too long to arrive or ordering a specialty product from a nearby store.[6] The employees also have the authority to use that budget to try new ideas. For example, if someone at a beachfront property realizes they could serve drinks more quickly with sand-adapted golf carts, they can order a golf cart and test their thesis.

Ideas that work get logged in an online innovation database so other locations can adopt the change.[7]

At Ideal Dental, we have adapted many of these programs and policies to our own needs. Every day offers an opportunity for each employee to practice serving customers, but we continually look for ways we can further reenforce our commitment by serving the community. For example, in partnership with retired Dallas Cowboys running back Emmitt Smith's charity, we regularly send several dental teams into underprivileged neighborhoods in Dallas to perform pro bono dental work. A lot of people who live in poverty struggle with inconsistent access to dental care. They might go years without seeing a dentist and often receive substandard care when they do. We worked on some kids who had already lost their baby teeth and then lost a few of their adult teeth too. They were afraid of smiling at school because they would get picked on. We replaced their missing teeth for free. There were elderly people without any teeth, and we fashioned them dentures. I could go on. The point is that whenever we serve the community, we make a huge impact, and all the dentists and assistants who volunteer say it's one of their favorite days of the year. It reminds them why we do we what do: to eliminate people's pain and help them get healthy and feeling better about themselves.

Adapt to Challenges

"Neither snow nor rain nor heat nor gloom of night stays these couriers from the swift completion of their appointed rounds." These words, taken from *The Persian Wars* by Herodotus, are set in stone above the entrance to the Eighth Avenue post office in New York City. This has become the unofficial motto of the USPS, and it perfectly encapsulates what I mean by adaptability. In a service culture, workers don't shrink from crises. They recognize that they have a noble and essential task. They rise to challenges with resilience and flexibility and do whatever they can to ensure the quality of their service doesn't slip.

One of the moments when I saw Ideal Dental show a lot of adaptability was at the start of the coronavirus pandemic. Our first response was to shut down our offices until we better understood the virus and the risks it posed. While dentists already take as many precautions as possible to stop the spread of respiratory illnesses, the nature of our work (practically leaning into a stranger's mouth) posed elevated risks during COVID-19. We took a significant financial hit, and I knew we would have to sacrifice to survive the pandemic. To make sure the top leadership led by example, I stopped paying myself, and most senior executives did as well or took a significant pay cut. We put off furloughs for as long as possible, and when we did need to furlough employees, we tried to keep that number to a minimum. When it was all said and done, we furloughed less than 10 percent of our employees.

We stayed closed for several months, doing our best to prevent the spread. But the country soon faced a web of interconnected crises. As COVID-19 infections spread, hospitals and emergency rooms quickly became overwhelmed. At the same time, people either couldn't or didn't want to go to the dentist. But toothaches and dental emergencies didn't stop. Since people avoided going to the dentist more than usual, those health problems got progressively worse. Eventually, people showed up at the emergency room with tooth pain. This, obviously, put even more pressure on the overtaxed medical system. It also created a worse outcome for the dental patients. The ER charges more, often for worse dental work. It became clear we needed to help relieve the pressure on hospitals, so we asked our staff to voluntarily return to the office to handle emergency procedures. This was still early in the pandemic, when New York City was relying on refrigerated trucks to store bodies and many Americans were bleaching their groceries.

Over 80 percent of our staff volunteered to return to work. They knew the risks, but they cared more about keeping people out of pain and out of the ER. Many of the people who didn't come back to work either were immunocompromised or lived with or took care of someone who was. Their willingness to take this risk is even more impressive when you consider they didn't stand to make a lot of money. Dentists get paid by the procedure—since we only offered emergency services, most of the dentists who came back worked limited schedules. They didn't do any cosmetic procedures or routine checkups that would usually fill up their schedules; therefore, they made less money than they did before the pandemic. Out of all that Ideal Dental has accomplished as a company, this is one of the moments I'm most proud of. It encapsulates our entire service ethos. When you make service the core of the business's culture, everything else seems to have a way of working itself out.

This is a major example, but a culture of service allows for countless smaller day-to-day adaptations. Our hygienists, dentists, and front office staff regularly work a little later in the day than staff at other practices to accommodate a guest in severe pain who can't reach our office until five o'clock. We also monitor all our stores to make sure the conditions allow staff to consistently serve their clients. When we find that a store can't maintain our standard, we rapidly adapt. For example, if a store gets booked for two or more months, we increase our capacity. If there's space in the office, or in the same building as the office, we hire new dentists, install new chairs and new equipment, and rapidly expand so we can get guests in and out faster. In the meantime, or if that's not an option, we send overflow patients to nearby sister offices.

Part of what makes this possible is our access to resources. When we need a dentist to cover for a colleague who can't come in, it helps to have hundreds of dentists on staff. During the COVID-19 pandemic, this turned into an even greater advantage. We could easily secure PPE in bulk for our workers and patients. We rapidly developed and implemented infection control in all our locations, including stickers measuring six feet of social distance and glass shields at reception. We had the capital and infrastructure in place to continue paying our employees during shutdown and attorneys who helped us structure furloughs when necessary. All this helped our dentists feel safe enough to return to work to see patients in pain, and helped put those patients at ease when they came in. We could also advertise about when we reopened and communicate clearly all the steps we'd taken for everyone's safety.

In short, we could respond more quickly and thoroughly than almost any solo dentist. Word got out about our response, and we started to attract new patients and even new dentists who wanted to join our community.

Part of what made this successful was our service ethos, which I made sure to incorporate into the core of our business from the very beginning. When we had a couple of offices, even after I stopped practicing dentistry to work on the business, I would still scrub up and take over if we had dentists who couldn't make it. Now that we have grown, I still tell people I'm willing to scrub up, although it happens much less often. More commonly, I have to plug other holes as they come up, and make sure I'm always available to respond to problems as they arise. This service culture can only come from the leader. You cannot ask people to be willing to put in the extra effort, to work longer, to work harder and faster, to give up their Friday golf rounds, if you're not willing to do it yourself.

Practice Transparency

Uncertainty and secrets sow fear and jealousy, both of which can erode a culture and lead to unproductive infighting and dissatisfaction. For example, if two people are both up for a promotion but neither knows how well they're performing, whoever doesn't get the promotion will be hurt and confused. They will fill the narrative vacuum with their own story. They might assume their boss holds a grudge against them or the person who got promoted undermined their case. This will lead the passed-over employee to sink energy into the black hole of office politics. Instead of focusing on their job, they'll dream up ways to "play the game." Or they might think something like, "Well, obviously the bosses just don't like me because of my no-nonsense attitude, so why try?" In that case, they will become disengaged. Either way, their productivity will drop. For that reason, we make three things very clear to everyone in our company: how they're performing, the criteria we use to award promotions, and why we decide to promote any given employee. As much as possible, we base this off data. Everyone has key performance indicators and scorecards that track their performance relative to expectations, with patient outcomes carrying the most weight. When we announce a promotion, we directly cite those metrics as well as the qualitative data we collect from peer evaluations that speak to emotional intelligence and leadership skills. This establishes a clear sense of what everyone who wants to advance needs to do. It also proves to everyone that interoffice subterfuge won't move their personal needle and, if anything, will hurt their chances of advancing. It all adds up to an amicable culture where people trust their teammates and feel motivated to collaborate instead of compete.

Work Hard to Play Hard

Humans are social beings. As much as we find meaning in our work, we still need to have fun and form a community with our colleagues, to take the time to celebrate a job well done and just have some good old-fashioned fun. It boosts morale and collaboration and helps retain key talent. At Ideal

Dental, we sponsor several large-scale events (although we paused them during COVID-19). For example, every year we host a gala, which more than one thousand people, including hundreds of employees, attend. We bring in interesting and accomplished speakers. Perhaps the most notable speaker was Emmitt Smith, the NFL running back mentioned earlier.

We also hold an all-company conference every year in Dallas, where employees come to learn from each other in a joyful environment. In 2020, the Dallas Cowboys cheerleaders, dance squad, and marching band kicked off our conference, while aerial acrobats performed in front of the stage. We also always build time into our conference schedules to allow teams to meet at a local restaurant for lunches and dinners—on us, of course—so everyone can bond and get to know their colleagues outside of a work setting.

Naturally, these conferences aren't just huge parties. We also use them to help reenforce our service culture. We hold training sessions about a wide range of topics from new advances in dentistry to what exemplary customer service means. We invite representatives from companies with outstanding customer service records to share their wisdom with us. We've been fortunate to learn from some of the best. For example, we brought in a speaker from Southwest Airlines. A quick YouTube search yields countless examples of Southwest's unparalleled culture. The videos depict flight attendants devising elaborate games to entertain passengers stuck on the tarmac and adding their unique humor and flair to preflight announcements. In all, we try to represent a cultural pinnacle, a deep commitment to service, and empowered, adaptable employees.

MARKET THE BRAND

Once you have the brand's core culture firmly in place, you can turn to the more superficial aspects of branding. If you've truly invested in an exceptional culture and customer experience, then this part is easy. You know exactly what you can offer that nobody else can, and you know what image you want to project to the world. All you need to do is communicate that core in a memorable, interesting way. To do that, I recommend you start with two key steps: clearly define your value proposition and create a uniform experience.

Define Your Value Proposition

A value proposition is a short statement that describes why a customer should choose you over your competitors. For example, our value proposition at Ideal Dental is that we guarantee the most convenient, safest, highest-quality dental work imaginable. Put simply, we are the ideal dentist. We design all our media (including taglines, logo, mailers, digital ads, and TV ads) as a riff on our value proposition.

I started developing our value proposition when I was opening my first offices. I had already come up with the name during an impromptu parking lot brainstorm, when I just kept saying over and over, "I just want everything to be ideal. An ideal guest experience." And it suddenly clicked. I knew I wanted to make a national brand, so I hired a firm to design a logo. The company was young, so I couldn't afford to invest a lot in branding. I got what I paid for.

The firm pitched a bunch of logos that all seemed as if someone had punched *Ideal Dental* into a template. I rejected the suggestions and decided to design the logo myself. I first chose the colors—mint green to make people think about the fresh feeling of just-brushed teeth, and a standard black. I made *Ideal* green and then moved on to the font. I wanted the font to more or less disappear, to draw extra attention to the words and colors. I went through several iterations until I found the most readable, most welcoming font. And that was it. I ended up with a logo that communicated what made our company unique: You will enter a calming environment and leave feeling refreshed, healthy, and happy. It also caught the eye far more than what the consultants had pitched. As we've grown, we've brought in firms to tweak the logo and make it look more modern and professional. But we still use the same core idea to guide our design.

As we built the rest of our communication strategies, we ensured they all aligned with the same core idea. For example, one of our taglines is "For all of your smile needs. Now that's ideal." We riff on that tagline by calling our 3D mouth-imaging services a 3D smile assessment. We do the same in our TV and online advertising. One of my favorites features a young boy skateboarding around his neighborhood on a weekend. He falls and chips his tooth. We then see him with his mother in an Ideal Dental waiting room, and a voiceover says, "Having a dental emergency on a Saturday? Not ideal. A dentist that's open six days a week? That's Ideal." And then we have a shot of them heading to their car after the appointment wearing giddy grins with the Ideal Dental building and logo in the background.

Back to my point, though, about culture. Cool as it is, that ad would be a hollow insult if any patients, once they got to our offices, had a subpar experience.

Create a Uniform Experience

Logos and media aren't the only ways to communicate with customers. Your physical and digital spaces, and how you design them, also send a message. I recommend you make sure that every detail of both works to convey the exact message you want and that they're the same across every office. For example, at Ideal Dental we want to create a comfortable environment that reminds people of home. A place where a kid feels comfortable playing and where they might expect a plate of hot cookies. To that end, we chose real stone countertops that look like they were pulled out of a kitchen; bright, non-fluorescent lights to lend everything a golden glow; and light, neutral-colored walls. Our employees all wear dark scrubs. We have Keurig coffee machines for people to have a beverage as they wait, and our waiting room has nice dark flooring, plush chairs, and often dark leather couches. The candles we buy usually have a vanilla or spiced scent to remind people of baking.

This uniformity principle extends to the digital realm as well. If our website had a black background and fancy-pants cursive lettering, it would make our bright offices look absurd. That website would convey a somber, exclusive air, the opposite of the welcoming vibe we want to project. On our website, we use a clean, white background with mintgreen lettering. A dark-themed website, to use a somewhat ridiculous example, would work for a dentist's office that catered to executives and charged exorbitant rates. For the interior of that business, I would choose darker wall colors, dim lights with fixtures that cast shadows, wooden trim around the doors, a cigar humidor, and private bar. Of course this would never happen, but you can imagine what that would feel like and why you would never take your children to get their teeth cleaned there.

CHAPTER

FIVE

Scale It Part 1: Start-Up to Midstage

We're all on a rocket ship, but we're building it as we fly. You can either help build it or get out. But either way, the ship has taken off."

I would tell my team that almost every day as we went from being a start-up to a midstage company. That's what it felt like at the time. I had to design the ship, keep our nose pointed moonward, and wield the wrench and blowtorch myself while supervising the entire construction.

Scary? Of course. Stressful? Precarious? Deeply. But in hindsight, these were some of the most fun and exhilarating parts of my life. An incredible energy surrounded the project. Everybody cared about their work and threw themselves into it. Each day I confronted a new challenge. Sometimes I succeeded, sometimes I failed, but I always learned.

And each day I got to see my grand vision become realized in the real world. What had only existed in my imagination became tangible.

To successfully build the rocket ship while hurtling toward the atmosphere, you need to focus on three areas: securing funding, hiring talent, and learning to manage and motivate people. I can't really give you a list of steps to follow, not only because each company is different, but also because each of those three areas is iterative. You will constantly need to grow as a manager, to make personnel changes, and to look for new funding. That being said, the most common growth pattern I see is getting more capital either from revenue, investment, or debt; needing to hire more people to expand or fill increased demand; and needing to learn how to run a larger company. Therefore, we will cover the areas in that order. But first I want to talk about habits that will help across all those areas: networking and maintaining relationships.

Strong relationships give you mentors to help navigate new challenges, connect you with potential lenders and investors to secure capital, and help you find and retain talent. They can introduce you to opportunities that you'd never find otherwise and help you gain traction in the company's early days.

NETWORKING AND RELATIONSHIPS

Everybody says it: your network is your net worth. And compelling empirical evidence backs this up. In 2022, the *New York Times* reported on a major study that identified interclass friendship as a key predictor of social mobility.[1] But I bristle at this standard interpretation of the axiom. People who buy into the network equals net worth equation seem to constantly search for higher net worth individuals to befriend. They only care about a person if they think that person can help them. This is not only callous, but it doesn't work, either. For a network to be an asset, the people in it need to want to see everyone in the network succeed, and that only happens if they feel a genuine connection.

You don't need to be everybody's best friend, but you should make an effort to have a meaningful relationship with the people you regularly interact with, whether they're employees or potential business partners. Doing so will enrich your life on many levels. Creating a wide network where everyone cares about one another often becomes more valuable than any business boost.

In my experience, there are four keys to successful relationship building: take (almost) every meeting, ask the right questions, be authentic, and maintain contact.

Take (Almost) Every Meeting

There's no such thing as a bad meeting. Just because someone can't help you in that moment doesn't mean that one day they won't have an opportunity to help you (or vice versa). Even as I've become busier, I make time to meet with a wide variety of people. They might be bankers, younger business people or dentists, real estate agents, business owners in other industries, or my employees.

In 2022, one of our dentists reached out to me. He was in his sixties and had worked for us for ten years. He'd received a terminal cancer diagnosis and couldn't work for us anymore, but he just wanted to talk. I made time for the meeting. I cared about him and his family. We didn't speak about business at all, but it was a chance for me to be there for him as a friend. Helping and supporting each other extends beyond the boundaries of our careers. I bring this mindset to all of my relationships, and it brings immense joy, richness, and depth to my life.

Ask the Right Questions

The biggest mistake most people make when networking is to focus on themselves. They only think about their needs, their struggles, and what they hope to get out of whomever they talk to. But good relationships are two-way streets. Showing genuine curiosity about everyone else's dreams, desires, aspirations, and struggles make them feel seen. They will like you more if you make them feel supported and valued. They are more likely to reciprocate, more likely to ask you what you want and need, and eventually you will find people whose interests or needs overlap with yours, people you can help while helping yourself.

A perfect example of this is our third dental office. That opportunity came because we were talking to my wife's friend who happened to be a dentist. She (the friend) was facing bankruptcy and wanted to sell her office before she had to file. That woman's struggle was an opportunity for both of us: we could help her avoid a major financial setback, and we could pick up a new office cheaply. As I mentioned in chapter 1, it took some time to turn the office around, but once we did, it became one of our top performers. This came about because we paid attention to the needs of the people around us.

Be Authentic

Some people, especially the hard-charging, hypercompetitive types, confuse authenticity with bragging or dominating conversations. If they receive pushback for their behavior, they claim, "I was just being myself." To me, that isn't authenticity. Outward displays of aggression and ego usually stem from a need to hide some fear or insecurity. Authenticity isn't acting on any given impulse. It's being honest about feelings, opinions, concerns, fears, insecurities, and, most importantly, desires. To build a fruitful relationship, people need to know what you want and what you're struggling with. If they don't, they can't help.

Throughout my entire career, I've told everybody I met that my goal was to create the Starbucks of dentistry. Most people dismissed me as unrealistic, but they all knew what I was trying to do. Likewise, I would communicate about my struggles. Maybe I was having trouble getting banks to give out more funding, or maybe I wasn't sure about where to look to open our next location. If you are too proud to admit you need help, you risk missing out on the best opportunities available. Because people knew my goals and struggles, they also knew how they could help me. And keep in mind that networking is a two-way street. When people help you, it's often because doing so can also help them. It's an opportunity for every party involved.

This dynamic led directly to many of my biggest early successes. For example, when I had about five offices, my banker called me to tell me about a challenge one of his other customers, a landlord, was having. Apparently, the landlord had financed a new dental office for a tenant in Sunnyvale, a small middle-class town outside of Dallas famous for their pecans. For a few months, everything was fine. Then the tenant stopped paying rent. The landlord couldn't reach the dentist, and when he went to visit, he found the office empty. The tenant had up and vacated without telling anybody. The landlord was stuck with $200,000 worth of debt in new dental equipment and a vacant office. They were hemorrhaging money and needed to fill the space as soon as possible.

I toured the location the same day I got the call, and it was the nicest office I had ever seen. They had sprung for all the nicest gear, including brand-new electric hand drills, each costing at least $5,000 retail. The ones we used at my other offices ran $1,500 and cut just a little bit slower. Even the location was perfect, chock-full of our ideal customer demographic. Still, I realized that taking on the note would be a risk. We would have to build the client list from scratch. Since our other offices were closer to Dallas proper, we didn't even have name recognition. Citing these challenges, I managed to get the landlord to lease use of the space for $6,000 a month, $2,000 less than his asking price. I took over $75,000 of the equipment debt, which the seller financed so I didn't pay a cent out of pocket. It was a win-win—I acquired an office with minimal risk, and the landlord found a tenant while spreading out their debt burden.

Before long, it became our best-performing office. Our overhead was lower than most of our offices, where we need to do about $40,000 a month to break even. At this office, because the lease was cheap and we didn't finance all the equipment, we broke even at $30,000 a month. Then, because I still had the time, I decided to work out of this location two days a week. That brought our overhead down to $20,000 a month. It didn't take long for us to smash past that number. The customers wanted all sorts of treatments, and word quickly got out about our exceptional service. By the time I brought in my first capital partner, I was comfortably profiting about $70,000 to $80,000 per month. It was a cash cow for which I had paid essentially nothing. As of this writing, that one office is valued at about $6 million.

And this all came about because my acquaintance at a bank knew exactly what I wanted to do and liked me enough that when he found an opportunity, he called me first.

Maintain Contact

Relationships require effort, but they require less effort than most people assume. In fact, as you become busier and your network expands to include other busy people, less effort becomes more impactful. Busy people don't have time to field hundreds of friendly drop-in texts or long phone calls. They often barely have time to bond with their families. A simple message every six months or so, especially tied to something specific, goes a long way. If I drive past a restaurant that makes me think of someone, or fly over their city in an airplane, I'll send them a quick message. Just a note that lets them know they're in my thoughts, maybe asks for a quick update, and wishes them well. If the stars align and I end up in their city with an opening at a mealtime, I'll ask them to meet up. If they ever come across an opportunity for me, or vice versa, the relationship is strong enough for us to connect and help each other.

SECURE FUNDING

Any business requires capital to grow. For the most part, there are three ways to get it: by self-funding, through debt, and by taking on investors. At this initial stage of the scaling process, I recommend leveraging debt as the primary funding stream. My ability to leverage debt was a huge part of how I was able to build a business in eight years that's now valued at over $500 million.

A lot of people, and many early business owners, shy away from debt. It stresses them out, and for good reason. Taking on debt is always a risk that makes you beholden to someone else. But it has its advantages. For starters, it is far less risky than using personal cash. If a self-funded business goes under, the owner will lose every last cent they invested. On the other hand, if a business that carries debt goes bankrupt, then the lenders will liquidate the business's assets, often leaving the founder's personal wealth more or less untouched.

Granted, taking on investors poses the least risk of the three options. But it puts a hard cap on how much money the founder can make. Every time a founder takes on outside capital, they sell off a portion of their company. If they start selling too soon, they'll be selling shares at the lowest price because their ownership gets watered down as the years go on. By the time they manage to build a large, high-value company, they might only own a sliver of it and lose out on the windfall that their hard work should have earned.

So start with taking on debt, but first learn how to leverage it. In my experience, there are two keys to growing by leveraging debt: take on smart debt, and diversify your debt burden.

Take on Smart Debt

Not all debt is created equal. Loosely, I divide debt into two categories: productive debt and hindering debt. Productive debt is any borrowing that directly covers an expense that will generate income, like adding a dental chair or building a new office. Hindering debt does not contribute to earnings. This might seem like common sense—only pay for what you need! But far too many businesses take on significant hindering debt.

For example, I've met several dentists who make it a point of pride to own their buildings, which usually requires them to take out a loan of somewhere between $500,000 and $1 million. This has advantages: they don't have to worry about unexpected rent hikes and more often than not the property will appreciate in value. For the most part, however, that's nonproductive value. It doesn't contribute to liquidity unless the owner takes out even more debt against the property's accrued equity. But more damning than that is the opportunity cost. For the same amount of money, they could renovate and open three or four leased offices. If properly run, each of those offices could turn into liquid currency machines, money that they can both reinvest and borrow against to spur further growth.

To be fair, owning the building might make sense if the founder only wants to own a couple of offices. If you want to scale, however, it will ultimately hurt your leverage. The lesson is to maintain maximum flexibility. For the most part, don't buy what you can lease for less money. And never ever take on debt for something that isn't 100 percent necessary to the business.

Diversify Your Debt Burden

Once we got through the challenging early days of expansion and started to turn a profit, I was raring to go. In about 2010, we had proof of concept, and my vision of creating the Starbucks of dentistry was closer to a reality than ever before. For the next couple of years, I opened as many offices as I could as quickly as possible. Then in 2012, the bank I worked with cut off my new funding because I was growing faster than their business model could fund. Remember, this was during the long, slow recovery from the 2008 recession. The media and politicians were publicly flogging financial institutions for their wanton lending practices. In response, banks adopted stringent lending standards, which made them twitchy about being overexposed in a single business.

At this point, I could only think of two ways to raise more capital. I could invest some of the money I had managed to save while growing the business, or I could look elsewhere for loans. The first option seemed far riskier, and far more selfish, than the others. I had a family I needed to look after. If I put up my own money, I would put our entire financial future at risk. New loans, on the other hand, would be attached to the business. It had always been my goal to grow the business without investing my personal wealth, so I went to other banks. I traipsed to a string of meetings and kept getting turned down. Eventually, I found a bank willing to extend more credit. I opened as many offices as I could with them until that well dried up too.

By now, my confidence was growing. We had our systems down to the point where it didn't take long for each new office to run at a profit, and

I saw no reason to stop. Since most of the national bank brands in Dallas had already turned me down, I started going to credit unions and smaller regional banks. These institutions enjoy far fewer business opportunities than the largest brands, and they can be more willing to take a risk, especially on a local entrepreneur. I found more capital there, and opened offices until, once again, I got cut off.

I spent a couple of weeks disappointed and discouraged. I didn't want to lose momentum, so I racked my brain for ways to continue to grow. Then I made a realization: I could bifurcate the incurred debt of opening each office. Each office cost about $300,000 to $400,000 to open. About half of that came from constructing the office—that's what I needed the banks for. The other half came from buying the equipment, but I could finance the equipment with the retailers. Even better, retailers offered better terms than banks, since were we to default, they could always repossess the gear, refurbish it, and then sell it again. The bank, on the other hand, would have to repossess and liquidate the gear, which carries a much lower price tag than reselling it directly to someone who needs it. Once I figured that out, I was able to lower my ask to a number that more banks were willing to lend me.

With new funding, you can go out and grow, which means you need to hire the right new talent.

HIRE THE RIGHT TALENT

In the last chapter we talked about hiring for culture. In this one we will talk about hiring the people with the right skills to help you grow. This is the single most important part of scaling, and while hiring is always important, who you hire matters most during the start-up phase. In a small company, a single bad apple can quickly rot the entire operation. Larger corporations with more established systems and cultures are more resilient, so one bad employee doesn't have the same degree of negative impact.

I see many founders struggle to hire. Part of this is because hiring can challenge the founder's ego. Being the sole decision-maker can be a huge burden, but it also confers a degree of status, and it ensures that the founder will never receive pushback against their decisions. In this period of my growth, I realized if I wanted to achieve all my goals, then I could no longer be content being the most qualified person in every "room" of my business. I recognized that in some arenas I needed to cede control to people with greater expertise and know-how. I needed to build a team that I could trust to work without my direct supervision.

In most businesses, the types of employees you need to hire fall into three main categories: expert talent, frontline and support talent, and business talent. Each one requires a different approach to attract and retain the best possible candidates.

Expert Talent

These are the experts, often highly trained, who develop and design new products or who execute a company's core service. In my business, these are the dentists. If I owned a software company, the experts would be coders. If I were a physical therapist, they would be the other physical therapists. Because these experts have the most direct control over product quality, companies often get into outright bidding wars for top performers.

During the start-up phase, you likely will lack the resources to win those bidding wars and will need to find a different way to attract the best experts. The way we did that was to turn our start-up status into a strength. Being a start-up allowed us to create a fun service culture that gave all our employees a great sense of purpose and a high degree of freedom, which we emphasized in our recruiting. We also emphasized that our top performers were provided a chance to buy equity in the company. This was a have-your-cake-and-eat-it-too offer. If they went into private practice, they would have to work clinically and handle all the other aspects of the business, such as the staffing, taxes, and marketing. We handled all that for them while giving them a shot at partial ownership and real wealth creation.

Of course, no matter how much you emphasize culture, you will still lose out on some of the most qualified candidates early on. That's why I recommend investing in creating your own crop of top performers. Even the top young doctors coming out of school don't know everything they need to excel in clinical practice. Many of them are like I was: confident because they don't even know yet how clueless they really are. To that end, we created an Ideal Dental mentoring program.

We pair each young dentist we hire with one of our top-performing dentists. The veterans mentor the newbies, teaching them about the unique Ideal Dental processes and making sure they can expertly execute every procedure we need them to. We also created a formal hands-on clinical training program, somewhat like a boot camp, that every new hire dentist goes through.

Once you've become more established, you can also ramp up your ability to recruit from the top training facilities in your field. For example, I have developed relationships with administrators and faculty at several elite dental schools. Each year we send a representative to give a presentation about our company to the schools. These are never sales pitches—just descriptions of what we do and what makes us unique. Likewise, we send reps to professional conferences to help build relationships with young dentists. Most of these young doctors are on the verge of entering the lifetime grind of a private dentistry practice. We offer them a chance to become a part of something bigger, and many jump at it.

Support Talent

When I say support talent, I am, for the most part, talking about hourly employees who don't have much highly specialized training. These employees either handle the product, work to support the expert talent, or act as a liaison between the customer and the company. For example, a warehouse worker who deals with inventory or a point-of-sale worker like a barista at Starbucks. In my business, our front office staff falls into this category.

These jobs matter. While the people who hold them usually don't have a college degree, they're anything but unskilled. Not everyone can be a great receptionist or barista or floor sales agent. Undervaluing these employees is a critical error, especially when they have a customer-facing role. These workers often make the first contact with customers. When a new patient visits Ideal Dental, they talk to the receptionist at least twice—once on the phone and once in the office—before they even see the hygienist, much less the dentist. If a front office employee speaks in a disrespectful or surly tone, makes frequent scheduling errors, or seems flustered, it creates a negative first impression. That first impression sets the guest's expectations for the rest of their visit, and the rest of the team will have to work extra hard to overcome it. Unfortunately, sometimes it can't be overcome. The damage is done.

The goal is not just to hire the best people, you'll also want to retain them. A lot of companies make the mistake of treating employees at this level as expendable. Amazon has received a lot of public heat about the conditions in their warehouses and how they treat frontline employees. This treatment results in turnover rates that are so high that some of Amazon's top executives actively worry about running out of new people to hire.[2]

Even so, while some mega-companies like Amazon can afford to churn through workers, constant turnover presents real risks and real costs. Training programs require significant investment, and a new employee often produces less and makes more mistakes until they have a firm grasp on their role. This is why it's vital you create an environment that will help you attract and retain top talent.

In my experience, the best frontline talent considers three factors when choosing an employer: compensation, culture, and opportunities for growth. They won't work for minimum wage when they can make more elsewhere. In every market we enter, we offer a higher starting wage for front office staff than our competitors do. Then we maintain a fun, respectful culture where everyone has a sense of purpose. We make it a priority to show respect to every applicant. I started this practice back when I made all the hiring decisions, and it's worked so well for us, it continues to this day.

Respect Every Applicant

One way to show respect is to respond promptly. If you've never applied for a frontline job, it can be difficult to comprehend the power of this small gesture. I know intelligent, hardworking people who have applied for jobs working the counter at a coffee shop or the check-in desk at a gym. They sent out dozens, if not hundreds, of applications. Often these applicants only receive an automated email thanking them for applying but never hear about a decision.

I can't tell you how many companies collect applications and keep people waiting on ice for days, if not weeks, before they respond, if they respond at all. Sometimes they don't even send an automated thank you. In my view, this is a surefire way to lose the best candidates.

Our approach is different, and it sends candidates a clear message: we care about our employees as much as we care about our clients. When I first started out, I posted our customer-facing job openings on websites like Craigslist. The applicants emailed me directly, and I always responded within twelve to twenty-four hours. Sometimes I would read an application and call the applicant within an hour of receipt to ask if they could do an interview that same day.

I hold my recruitment and hiring team to this same standard. If they start to take longer than twenty-four hours to respond I drop in to refocus them on our expectations. Several times this team has pushed back or claimed it is impossible to respond to every applicant so quickly. But I reminded them that I did it alone for several locations while I also practiced dentistry and handled other aspects of the business such as negotiating with banks and builders and running advertising campaigns. Plus I didn't have the benefit of the specialized software we've provided for our teams. If I could respond to applicants right away under those conditions, then so can they, and they almost always do.

Seek to Promote from Within

Once we have a new hire, we continue to show how much we care, largely through orienting them to our internal training and advancement programs. Another way we treat people with respect is we always seek to promote from within before recruiting from outside.

For frontline employees who want to enter management, we offer specialized training. There is virtually no limit to how high a motivated employee can climb. One of our top executives started as a front desk worker. It's the old-school American dream–type opportunity, which has become a rarity. But it's alive and well at Ideal Dental, and all our employees know it.

Business Talent

Business talent covers anyone who works in a field universal to all businesses like marketing, operations, sales, supply chain, legal, accounting, and acquisitions. Most young businesses make these hires gradually—a marketing person this month, an operations manager the next. The order varies from business to business, although I do recommend filling one position before anything else: finance and accounting.

Unless you're an accountant, do not file business taxes on your own, especially during a period of rapid growth. The stakes are just too high. If you develop and roll out a bad ad campaign, it might cost a lot of money, but you can recover from that. If you make a lot of errors on taxes, you could land in a legal quagmire. And you will make mistakes. As a business grows, it becomes subject to exponentially more complicated regulations and tax policies. The more income you generate, the more debt you carry, the more you pay out in expenses, all of this requires specialized knowledge and consistent attention to ensure you meet your obligations and protect yourself against other potential threats such as government regulation crackdowns or internal issues like embezzlement or other types of theft.

After handling finance, your individual strengths and the company's needs determine when you fill other positions. Many start-up entrepreneurs do everything: run operations, oversee supply chain, manage multiple branches, develop and execute ad campaigns, make operational improvements. Each time they hire someone, they get to fire themselves from that job.

To understand what positions you need to hire first, make an honest assessment of your capabilities. What are your greatest business strengths? Your greatest weaknesses? What tasks inspire energy and joy, and which ones feel like a slog? And, most importantly, in which roles can you generate the most value for your business? Your answers will determine what roles you need to fill and how you should organize your company.

In my own example, my strengths have always been in two areas: my ability to connect with people and my capacity to develop a grand vision and execute it. This makes me much more of an operational leader than anything else. We already talked about the first job I fired myself from: dentistry. I brought on several dentists and made one of my early partners, Dr. Shalin Patel, the chief medical officer. It's Dr. Patel's job to keep up with new developments in dentistry and train all the doctors in contemporary best practices. This allowed me to dedicate all my time to leading and running the company.

I cannot stress this enough: in the vast majority of cases, the first job you need to fire yourself from is that of your own area of expertise. Growing a business takes an all-consuming amount of work. To succeed, you need to dedicate yourself to working *on* the business, not *in* the business. This requires a leap of faith. Most expert entrepreneurs are great at what they do and find their work rewarding. They also, especially in the lean early days of a company, earn most of their income from plying their craft. Most people want to give up this job last, and that's a big part of why most people fail to scale their businesses.

As we grew, I jettisoned more of my job titles. Because I never grasped the nuances of digital marketing and search engine optimization, I hired people for those tasks. Then I started to hire people who could handle employment decisions for me, and so on. For the longest time, I kept most of the operations roles myself. I scouted possible locations, secured funding, and negotiated with contractors and suppliers. Once I had competent people or teams running the rest of the business, and once we grew to a point where I couldn't handle operations on my own anymore, I started to hire people to help with these tasks.

Contrast this with someone I know who runs a corporate consulting company. This man is a genius business consultant. He has a unique philosophy and a knack for asking the right questions and helping his customers discover opportunities. He has other consultants who work for him, but they all teach a variation of his philosophy. He is in high demand and charges a premium for his services.

When he tried to scale, he started to work on the business more than in the business. He took on fewer clients, spent less time training the other consultants and overseeing their work, and spent more time thinking about such things as strategy, sales, recruiting, streamlining internal communications and processes, and advertising. His company's growth became erratic, and customer satisfaction slipped. He had, unwittingly, pulled out the very core of his business. The company's successes had depended on his personal skill. Also, in a bizarre bit of irony, this genius consultant is a weak manager. He thrives on helping people identify and solve problems. When it comes to implementation, he's a bit hapless.

The business puttered on for a while until the founder recognized that something needed to change. He asked one of his consultants—an operations expert—to take over as managing partner so he, the founder, could devote more time to working in the business. He took on the role of president and went back to overseeing other consultants' work while developing business plans with the managing partner. He could still exercise his strategic brilliance but had someone he could trust to implement the new initiatives. Soon after that shift, the business, and the impact they had, rapidly expanded.

Once you've hired the staff, you need to make sure the new team members execute their tasks to the level you've set. Usually this requires a lot of growth from founders, many of whom are experts in their field but have little or no management training or experience. At this point, you must become a manager. Chapter 6 covers in-depth one of the most important parts of training employees and holding them accountable to high performance standards. For now, I want to explain a bit about my guiding management strategy.

IT'S YOUR BABY: A CASE FOR MICROMANAGING

Almost all business books published in the last ten or fifteen years argue against micromanaging. They contend that micromanaging saps morale and reduces employee creativity. In certain contexts, I agree. As a general rule the bigger a company gets, the greater the risks that overmanagement will impede growth, mainly because there are so many managers and bureaucratic legacy processes to follow.

During the start-up phase, however, undermanagement poses a far greater threat. In this phase, everything changes constantly. New locations open. Vendors change. Customers and employees come and go, and revenue expands or shrinks rapidly. Challenges you would have never anticipated arise every day, and you'll have to develop a system to handle them. You will also need to develop the processes that allow you to deliver your product or service from scratch, which often requires hundreds of rounds of testing and tweaking. It will take all your effort to pay adequate attention to each part of the business.

A lapse in attention can prove catastrophic. Take, for example, Chobani yogurt.[3] In the early 2010s they grew so fast that the leaders were unable to monitor production and ensure quality, which resulted in the distribution of sizeable amounts of tainted yogurt in 2013. This led to at least one recall and a resulting PR crisis that threatened to undo everything they'd accomplished. The situation got so bad that the board considered replacing the founder/CEO with an operations expert known for turning around struggling companies. They opted to keep their CEO, and eventually Chobani was able to regain control over their product's quality and continued to grow and thrive.

The business is your baby. And just as with a real baby, an inattentive steward can prove fatal to your business. If you had a young child with a severe peanut allergy, you would micromanage the babysitter. You would give the babysitter a list of restaurants that didn't use peanuts and tell them to put the kid in a car seat during the drive. I recommend using the same approach with a start-up business. Give strict guidelines about all the important aspects of the business.

Set a high standard and hold everyone accountable. I call it a trust-but-verify approach. Once I've hired someone, I'm hands-on with them until I know they can do their job. Then I let them do it, occasionally checking in to make sure they are hitting all the metrics that we need. And if they start to struggle, I support them and help them get back on track. But if they can't, then we do what is ultimately best for us and them. We let them go.

There are, of course, countless other elements that go into effective management, foremost among them emotional intelligence, as we covered in chapter three. But an important, and often underdiscussed, aspect of leadership is making sure that you are in a place where you can succeed. If you succumb to pressure and burnout, then you're much more likely to make mistakes ranging from strategic blunders to unfairly lashing out at colleagues and direct reports. You need to take care of yourself and put yourself in a position to perform at a high level.

KEEP YOURSELF RUNNING

In this chapter we've covered perhaps the single most stressful time in a business's life cycle, essentially a company's infancy to toddlerhood. This phase of growth demands endless work, often with little to no pay. By the end of this stage, even if the "baby" is healthy, it's unstable and completely dependent on you to keep it safe and going in the right direction. In short, this stage has the potential to be the burnout zone.

To ensure you continue to feel the motivation to move forward, you must find ways to keep yourself happy, optimistic, and energized enough to serve your customers and employees. We all know the classic cure-alls for burnout: good sleep, exercise, hobbies, time with family, a healthy diet. This is all excellent advice, but I want to address how to combat burnout in a business context. The two most important ways are to pay yourself first and to celebrate successes.

Pay Yourself First

Many business owners resist this. They might even feel guilty for paying themselves when they could reinvest that cash into the business. This instinct, while admirable, is detrimental in the long run. Except for in moments of absolute crisis, you should pay yourself first. You're taking the risk, working the hardest, sleeping the least. You deserve a reward. And pursuing a grand vision is a long, strenuous process. It's a marathon that you have to sprint through. If you don't give yourself an indication that all the effort is paying off, you'll lack the strength to carry on when you need to most.

Celebrate Successes

Growing up in Zimbabwe, I kept a Ferrari calendar on my wall for over a decade after it expired. I loved the calendar, but there was one car in particular, a bright red number, that I loved most of all. I kept the calendar turned to that month for years just so that I could see it every day. One day, when I was about sixteen, I remember looking at that sun-faded picture. In that moment, I promised myself I would own a Ferrari before I turned thirty years old.

I came to the US, and after dental school I worked for someone else for a few years. When I started my own business, I was twenty-eight. Those first few years had been grueling, but just before I turned thirty, the business was finally making money. I wanted to reward myself for getting through this period, to value the effort I had put in, and to celebrate the success. Plus, I had a promise to keep.

I went to buy a Ferrari even though I couldn't quite afford it yet. My dad came with me because I needed someone to drive the old car back, and because I was a nervous wreck. In the showroom, I examined each car in minute detail about a million times. Finally I settled on a model F430 and sat at the dealer's table to make the purchase. But that close to the finish line, I couldn't make up my mind. I asked my dad incessantly what he thought. Then I waffled over the decision with the dealer. I wrung my hands over whether it was a wise investment. Each time I thought about making such an expensive purchase and pictured myself signing the contract, I remembered the night in the middle of December of 2009 when I had to use some of my dwindling money to cover payroll. Here I was at the end of 2010, barely a full year removed from my lowest point, contemplating a massive purchase. It felt like another low moment like December's was right around the corner, and this car would send me hurtling toward the bend.

I dithered so long that my dad fell asleep right in the uncomfortable dealership chair. I made the dealer recite his spiel again. About thirty minutes later my father suddenly jolted awake. When he realized I hadn't decided, he sighed and said, "If you're buying it, buy it now. Otherwise, we're leaving."

I bought it.

I settled into the driver's seat and paused to take everything in. The car was made of carbon fiber and black hand-stitched leather. The cockpit was snug, a hallmark of Ferrari's, and I felt cradled in its powerful shell.

Turning on the engine for the first time was visceral, exhilarating. I felt the vibrations from the engine travel through my arms and explode into my chest. I felt charged.

Still learning how to manage the car's power, I nudged the accelerator and felt the whole vehicle come alive. I navigated to the edge of the lot and turned onto the street, heading uptown. Night had descended, and I rode through the dark toward the skyscrapers with their blazing windows. I felt I had accomplished something, that all the fourteen-hour days and stress-filled nights had paid off. I knew there was a long way to go, but it felt like the company had all this horsepower, all this juice. All we had to do was open her up, and we would go roaring forward.

CHAPTER

SIX

Perfect Your Playbook

Toward the end of his life, groundbreaking physicist Albert Einstein wore the same gray suit every day. Apple founder Steve Jobs famously wore a black turtleneck every day. The renowned film and TV director David Lynch eats the same lunch and dinner each day: a piece of toast with chicken. For all these iconic figures, the same logic leads to these rigid ways: the fewer decisions they need to make, the more time and energy they can devote to their work.

Every small decision an employee has to make distracts from their work. Effective leaders eliminate small decisions so employees can dedicate their full time and energy to their work and search for innovations. When you can create this kind of work environment, anything is possible. Maybe your employees will discover your company's equivalent of the theory of relativity, iPhone, or *Twin Peaks.*

In my experience, the best way to limit employee decision-making is by creating playbooks that contain detailed instructions on how to execute each function. They also have another benefit: standardization and quality control. Quality of service usually peaks early in a company's life cycle. This is because the founder always cares more about the company's performance than anyone else. In the start-up phase, the founder's presence generates a special energy that animates the employees. As the company expands, that energy becomes more diffuse as it spreads across several locations. Newer hires feel a bit less connected and motivated than the founding core, and their work can reflect that gap. The best way to combat this natural slippage is to have a playbook for every role in your business. Not only will this help you run a better business, it also raises the value of your company. When someone invests in a company, a big piece of what they're buying is the playbooks, so the sooner you write your playbooks, the better.

WRITING AND USING THE PLAYBOOKS

The most important piece of advice I can give about writing playbooks is to pay attention to every single detail. Any step of the process that you leave unaccounted for will invite an employee to either neglect their duties or do whatever they feel like doing. When I wrote the first Ideal Dental playbooks, I had about three offices. I created a document for each employee and drafted a list of their roles. Then I wrote detailed steps for each role. No part of the process was too small. The receptionists' playbook included answering each phone call with, "Thank you for calling Ideal Dental. How can we make you smile today?" Then I wrote steps for how to handle each type of call (potential customer, first-time customer, returning customer, scheduling, rescheduling, insurance inquiry, care follow-up inquiry). At the end of the playbook, I listed every target metric for each role and included some warnings against mistakes I'd seen.

Our playbooks have evolved with our company. Now we periodically convene a group of our top-performing employees in each department and position to have them share their strategies with one another. Those meetings almost always result in a revised set of best practices, which we incorporate into the playbooks. Whenever something significant changes in the business, we edit and rerelease our playbooks to reflect the change.

Of course, the playbooks only matter if employees actually follow them. To that end, we have a classroom-style video learning interface called DECA Academy, where all our employees get trained in whatever playbook they need to learn and are later tested to confirm they've internalized the lessons.

There are seven essential types of playbooks that I recommend drafting: operational, sourcing and supply chain, location selection, office construction, hiring and training, marketing, and performance evaluation and metric reporting.

Operational Playbooks

The day-to-day operations of individual stores are covered in the operational playbooks. Ideally, the playbooks that you write for each employee's role will result in a tightly choregraphed dance that shows what to do at each step of the customer experience, and how and when to hand off the customer to the next person for the next step in the chain. To help you imagine playbooks in action, here's a brief example from my business.

It starts before the guest even calls. The playbooks go over how to set up the operatory for every possible interaction, such as a cleaning and consult, a root canal, or a filling. This means, for example, I could go tomorrow into any Ideal Dental location and perform any operation without looking at the tool tray because I know by heart the order in which the tools will be laid out.

Then there's a prescribed process for each type of customer. Let's say we get a walk-in complaining about tooth pain. The front staff would seat them in the operatory within five minutes of their arrival. The technician would then take an X-ray, 3D scan, and picture of their mouth. Those images would go to the dentist, who would review them. After that, the dentist would enter the operatory to introduce themself and ask some diagnostic questions. At that point, the dentist would have a diagnosis and begin to explain the issue to the guest. The playbook instructs the dentist to first show the patient their internal mouth pictures because patients can easily comprehend those. The dentist would say something like, "Here's where you have a hole in the tooth, and it goes pretty deep. You can see all the black stuff—that is decay."

Then the dentist would switch to the X-ray to explain what it means clinically. They would show where the decay is, how deep it goes into the gum, and where it hits the nerve. Then they would say something like, "It's too late. What you need is a simple procedure. I will go in, disinfect the nerve, then build the tooth back up and put a porcelain crown on top of it all."

That procedure is a root canal. But our playbook instructs dentists to explain the actions of the procedure before stating the name because when people hear something like *root canal*, they panic. They associate it with unbearable pain. But that's a myth—properly executed, there's nothing scary or excruciating about the procedure.

The guest would then probably ask about the cost of the procedure. The dentist would introduce the patient to the financial coordinator, who would break down the costs, the insurance information, and whatever payment options are available. Once the coordinator leaves, the dentist would return and finish the procedure within a set time limit. Then the guest would check out. Later that night, because the dentist numbed the guest's mouth, the dentist would call them to check on how they were feeling.

Each playbook indicates what we expect from each employee at each step and provides metrics that each employee has to hit. Every single step is timed, and if one step takes too long, our automated system flags that as a problem. This allows workers to flow seamlessly from one task to the next without having to scramble to catch up or to wait for the person in the chain before them to finish their work.

Sourcing and Supply Chain Playbooks

Our materials sourcing is what inspired me to draft our playbooks. I had just opened my fourth office and left each manager in charge of restocking our dental equipment. I still practiced at the time, and one day when I went to treat a guest, I couldn't find a tool I needed. A few days later, I went to work at a different location. That day I needed to take an impression of my guest's mouth, and we only had an inferior impression material in stock. A few days later, at another location, I noticed the staff using a subpar anesthetic. This made me realize how desperately we needed standardization. If I couldn't manage the details at four offices, how could we ever grow? I started with the sourcing playbook because it was one of the easiest to write and one of the most visible.

There are few things more embarrassing than having to tell a patient to come back because we ran out of crowns. I set out to ensure we had the highest-quality tools and didn't waste money on supplies we didn't need. I searched online for the most reputable vendor and then audited all our processes. I looked at data from each office to see how many guests we saw each week on average and how many of each procedure we performed. I listed everything we needed and the number of each item the manager should order per month as a baseline. Out of the over fifty thousand items the vendor offered, I ended up with a list of five hundred items. Managers can order any of those five hundred items whenever they need to, but they may not deviate from the master inventory list without special permission.

Location Selection Playbook

Thanks to our excellent playbooks, every store we open offers the same quality of service. In other words, we've controlled for every variable that determines profit, except for one: location. Our choice of location will make or break any office we open, so we cover how to pick the perfect spot in our location selection playbook. The core of that process is our regression model. As a little Statistics 101 lesson, a regression model measures the relationship between a dependent variable (in this case location income) and one or more independent variables.

To build the model we started with an understanding of cost. We knew that we wanted to build each location for about $350,000 and that we wanted to cap our monthly overhead at about $40,000 per location. This served two functions: first, it allowed us to rule out any location that would cost significantly more than our baseline. Second, it told us exactly how much revenue we would need to break even. That way, when we build out the rest of the model, we would be able to tell how long it would take for each potential location to become profitable as well as the maximum profit we could reasonably expect from each location.

That gave us the baseline. To build the predictive model, we looked at our past results. We examined our locations that had been open for at least three years (younger offices sometimes struggle to reach capacity) and charted how much revenue they generated in each quarter. Then we looked at location-specific data for each office, most notably median household income, the dentist to population ratio in the area, the rate at which the local population was growing, and what other businesses operated in the area. The logic behind the last one was simple. We try to open near a business that our ideal customer frequents (like a Whole Foods or Starbucks) so they see us as they go about their day, and so they can visit us while running other errands. I was also intentional about how I wanted to position our brand. I wanted us to be associated with other successful upscale companies, which was another reason I searched for locations near natural markets like Whole Foods. These spaces usually cost more per square foot than others, but I paid the premium because I knew it would help as attract guests, and I was right.

Once we settled on our independent variables (median income, number of dentists per capita, other businesses nearby), we made a separate scatter plot for each that looked at location revenue against the independent variable. Then we used our plots to write an equation that showed the relationship between the dependent and independent variables. (If you don't understand how to do this sort of analysis, hire someone who does.) That process gave us the foundational model we could use to predict location income.

Of course, as we grow we update and refine the model. To do that, we collect customer data and analyze their behavior and preferences. For example, our records show that the vast majority of our patients live no more than a seventeen-minute drive away. That bit of knowledge tells us which area to use to calculate our dentists per capita metric—we know to look for the number of dentists within a thirty-four-minute-drive radius from any prospective location.

And that's it. It's relatively simple statistical analysis. Now all we have to do is simply plug potential addresses into the model, and it tells us how well each hypothetical office will perform. Most of our competitors also use regression models. However, most of our competitors haven't standardized their operations as much as we have, which introduces other variables into the system. As a result, their models predict performance with only about a 30 percent accuracy. As of 2022, ours accurately predicted performance 81 percent of the time. This was the highest in the dental space and led us closer to our goal of accomplishing a standardized retail healthcare model.

Office Construction Playbook

Our goal is to open a store as quickly and a cheaply as possible without sacrificing quality. The first office I built from scratch cost $800,000. By 2022, we had refined the process to the extent that our average opening cost was only $350,000, not adjusted for inflation. We arrived at this number through a lot of experimentation. Early on, I tried a slightly different process with each office I opened until I landed on the perfect formula. I found there are five main ways to reduce costs and maximize efficiency: maximize space use, eliminate equipment redundancies, develop a rigorous bidding system, don't overspend on equipment and materials, and master the permitting process.

1. **Maximize Space Use:** Controlling for other factors like location, smaller spaces usually cost less than larger ones. Therefore, a great way to save money is to use less space. For example, in my first couple of offices, we put sinks in every single operatory. Not only did this use a lot of space, it cost a lot of money to buy individual sinks. Later, we switched to island sinks, which we embed into the divider that we place between operatories so two rooms can use the same sink. This reduces our overall space use and materials cost, saving an average of $6,000–$8,000 per office. Stay on the lookout for similar opportunities, and whenever possible consider reducing overall office space by emphasizing remote work.
2. **Eliminate Equipment Redundancies:** In my first new office, we put an X-ray arm into every single operatory. They each cost thousands of dollars, but I wanted to maximize convenience. This way, patients wouldn't need to wait for the machine to free up or even leave their operatory. However, I quickly noticed that X-rays don't take long, and not every guest needs X-rays. I figured there had to be a more efficient way and did some research. My

instinct proved correct—someone had invented a portable X-ray arm called the Nomad, which cost $6,000. We now buy one or two of those for each office (depending on the size of the office), which saves us more than $10,000 per office and still allows for maximum convenience. We ensure guests get X-rayed quickly without having to leave their operatory or moving their head to accommodate the X-ray arm.

3. **Develop a Rigorous Bidding System:** A good contractor is hard to find. It seems like most never finish a project on time or under budget. In my experience, the only way to find a good contractor is to deploy a rigorous bidding system and incorporate it into your playbook so employees know how to evaluate proposals.

   Before you even think about soliciting bids, start with a budget. Use your experience from opening previous locations in the area to get a sense of how much labor and materials should cost so you can negotiate from a position of knowledge and strength. If it's your first project, then do some research. Find someone who has gone through the process before and ask them what to expect, how to evaluate bids, and how to tell when a contractor is overpromising. If you can't find anyone, read online forums about working with contractors, look for reviews of local building companies, and seek out books on the subject. But keep in mind that we all have to start somewhere. Your first couple of times through the building process, you will probably make mistakes, just like I did (more on that below). The key will be to learn from them.

   Once you've done your prep, circulate the project announcement and evaluate the bids as they come in. Stress in the playbook that cheaper isn't always better. What matters is to determine the logic behind the proposal. If a contractor makes an offer that seems too good to be true, it probably is. For example, someone might claim they can finish the job while using two fewer workers than their competitors. That's a recipe for project delays. If you're expanding rapidly, you can leverage that growth to drive down this one cost since a contractor hired to work on several offices will most likely charge less per office.

Before you commit to a contractor require their references and a list of their current jobs. Talk to each reference and go to each worksite to observe. Are the builders working consistently? How many people show up? Does it look like this contractor uses solid materials? I also like to put in the contract that the contractor must send us weekly progress reports complete with pictures.

In our playbooks, we stress that the process doesn't stop once we've hired the contractor. When we were a start-up, I visited each worksite. Once I found a new location completely empty, and it looked like it hadn't been worked on in days. While there, I called the contractor and asked for an update. He told me, "Great! I have four guys on site putting caulk in as we speak."

I said, "That's interesting, because I'm here and I don't see anybody." We never used that contractor again. Since then, I remind my employees that this is the same as any other process. We need to trust but verify our contractors.

4. **Don't Overspend on Equipment and Materials:** I handled every aspect of opening my first office, so I spent a lot of time talking to salespeople. And a lot of them were good. I wanted to build the best office around, and they could sense that. They pushed me toward the most expensive products, and it worked. I bought the $12,000-a-unit dental chair because they would supposedly never break. And they didn't. But it took a long time to break even on that first $800,000 office, and I wondered if I could reduce our costs. So a few offices later I decided to try out the

$2,000 dental chairs. As it turned out, those never broke either, and they didn't look cheaper or work worse than the $12,000 chairs. More expensive isn't always better, but you won't know until you try the options.

5. **Master the Permitting Process:** In the United States, building and space-use permits are awarded at the local, not state, level. That means every jurisdiction has a different permitting process and requires different documentation at different times. And just as some businesses perform better than others, some cities have more efficient permitting offices. As you expand into new cities, update your playbook to include exactly what you need to submit to each city and at what part of the process. Use this to coordinate other deadlines (for example, if you need to submit blueprints eight weeks before you start building, have the blueprints ready at least two weeks before that). As you learn more about how that city's office works, translate that experience into new guidelines. For example, if you know that a particular city always experiences delays and doesn't release permits on time, make a note in the playbook to submit the application early and to continually follow up on the application status.

Hiring and Training Playbooks

New outposts need staff to run them. I recommend that your playbook include the timeline for staffing a new office and the best processes to follow to get it up and running. For example, at Ideal Dental we know that the hiring and training process takes about three months in total. So we post job openings in the new area and start looking for internal promotion candidates three months before opening. While every employee matters, the key to getting a new office off on the right foot is well-prepared leadership, so most of our playbook is dedicated to that. In our locations, the leadership is two key people: the office manager and the dentist. It is their job to ensure every employee embodies our Ideal ideals, puts the customer first, and treats everyone with care and empathy.

Our playbook instructs hiring managers to promote from within whenever possible. When we promote people, we give them management training before we put them into their new position. We want each location to launch with plenty of momentum and prefer to put a known leader at the helm. A bad leader in a new office does much more damage, and far faster, than a bad leader in an established one. We maintain a list of our top-performing assistant managers and front office staff who have indicated they want more responsibility.

We follow the same procedure for dentists. In each of our offices, we usually staff a primary dentist and at least one secondary dentist. For the most part, the primary dentist is more experienced and mentors the junior dentists. The added responsibility usually means more opportunities and more money. We have all our primary dentists report to us about their mentees, and from those reports we develop a list of high-performing junior dentists who want to run their own shop and stop playing second fiddle.

Once we've filled every role, we send everyone to DECA Academy, where they learn every playbook they need to know to perform their job. We always hire a few more people than we need because we often find that once we start the training process, some new hires will naturally drop out or reveal themselves to be a mismatch in our culture. After one or two months, we have a core workforce prepped and ready to make our new guests smile.

Marketing Playbooks

Loosely, I divide our marketing playbooks into two categories: launch marketing and general marketing. The specific details of each differ, but the process to generate both is the same. We rely on a suite of metrics that track how many new clients each campaign and type of marketing generates, and calculate our return on investment by campaign. Then we optimize according to those metrics.

We also use these metrics to build another regression model that shows which ads most effectively promote a new location and when we should start to roll out those ads. Our data shows it's easy to start advertising too soon. If we sign a lease and get the permits six months before we open, we usually don't start advertising until a month before opening. At that point, we put up our sign and send out a round of mailers. A week after that we start digital advertising within a three-mile radius. A week after that we increase the frequency in a two-mile radius, and in the last week before we open, we shower the mile around our new location with ads. According to our data, that strategy builds a wave of excitement that crests just as we open and sends the customers flooding in.

Performance Evaluation and Metrics Playbooks

If a company is like a child, the playbooks that focus on evaluation and reporting are the GPS smartphone technology that allows parents to track their teenagers. The playbooks outline how leaders keep track of the entire business, and they teach them how to identify problems before they fester and become crises. Evaluation and reporting are both essential to agility and quality control over sprawling enterprises. On a practical level, the playbooks detail which metrics to track, how to track them, who in the chain of command can access them, and how the information is used. While you will develop your own reporting processes, I've found that the most successful evaluation and reporting systems all do the same four things: zero in on the key performance indicators, automate metrics as much as possible, use internal net promoter scores, and encourage reflection.

1. **Zero In on the Key Performance Indicators:** Every day in the hallowed halls of America's universities, think tanks, lobby groups, business incubators, and trade groups, an army of brilliant people devote hours to developing new, complicated models that analyze business activities from any angle imaginable. This has only accelerated in the twenty-first century with a spike in MBA enrollment and the explosion of undergraduate business programs. The result: you can now track almost anything you want and segment data more than ever before. We are drowning in metrics. And while a lot of the newer, more complicated analyses might be useful, they most certainly are complicated.

   I love to do a deep dive into metrics but always with the goal to cut through the noise and identify the data that actually drives performance. As such, I've highlighted a few metrics, known as key performance indicators, you need to track to actually move the needle. As soon as possible, figure out what those metrics are for your business and track them obsessively. In my business, I look for the numbers that directly contribute to customer satisfaction and revenue. Those are the two things that matter most.

   For customer satisfaction, we track our customer net promoter score, our total wait time, wait time at each part of the process, our rework rates (what percent of our completed operations require rework), and average Google review rating by location. Of course, this is the top line, and each department and region tracks metrics that feed into these.

   For example, let's take the new guests topline metric. Each individual location obviously tracks their new guests per week and month. At the same time, our advertising team tracks digital advertising engagement (clicks) in each region, and the conversion rate from click to client. They also track the percentage of new clients that come from each advertising strategy and the percentage of first-time clients who become repeat clients. Every smaller indicator we track in some way feeds into the top-level indicators we track, and they all directly affect revenue and satisfaction.

In the revenue realm, we track such metrics as number of new guests overall, sales per location, sales per day, return on investment for advertising, overall costs, itemized expenses, and productivity per chair.

The earlier you begin tracking your most important metrics the better. It will get you into the habit of using these numbers to make informed decisions. Plus the more robust an early reporting infrastructure you build, the easier it will be to automate your reporting systems as you scale.

2. **Automate Metrics as Much as Possible:** This piece of advice becomes more essential as you grow. All the metrics you want to track can be easily automated and plugged into a real-time digital dashboard that will allow you to access the most up-to-date numbers at each location any time you want to. But that can be a significant investment and usually is only worth the cost once you have scaled to a point you can't easily track metrics at each location with manual reporting methods.
3. **Use Internal Net Promoter Scores:** This metric is just like a regular net promoter score but for our employees. So instead of asking our customers whether they would recommend us to their friends and family, we ask our employees if they would recommend us as an employer, and we give them a chance to share any other thoughts. We keep the responses confidential, but we do track what location and department each employee works in. The goal is to have as high a score as possible because when you have happy employees, it almost always translates to happy customers. These metrics also

give us valuable information about our leaders' emotional intelligence. If, for example, after we make a new hire or promotion we notice that everyone reporting to that person suddenly becomes unhappy at work, that raises a red flag. We can investigate to see if the manager is upholding our cultural values. Also, we can use these metrics to help us decide who gets promoted.

4. **Encourage Reflection:** The fastest way to ensure an employee develops is through reflection, when they take the time to evaluate their performance on their own. When employees reflect on their work, they develop a better understanding of the challenges they face, the opportunities they may have missed, their weaknesses, and their strengths. In doing so, they can refine their behavior, and sometimes this leads to innovative ways to execute their jobs. At the bare minimum, I recommend quarterly performance reviews where employees can evaluate their performance in a conversation with a manager.

   To take a step further, look for ways to build a reflection mechanism into everyone's day-to-day routine. For example, I've always instructed my direct reports to email me a summary of their day every day. When I had just a few locations, those were the office managers, and they included their write-ups with their reports of metrics such as how many guests we served and our revenue. Now it's my executive team, including the C-suite and VPs. I tell them to include what they did, why they did it, the outcome, the challenges they encountered, and their next steps.

   The *why* question is the most important part of the email. It's what encourages them to reflect, and it helps me evaluate their mindset and prioritization and decision-making skills. Everyone who reports to me has more on their plate than they can finish. I need them to always focus on the actions that will make the biggest impact. Because of these emails, I can direct everyone's energy toward the projects that keep us charging forward.

CHALLENGES TO STANDARDIZATION

No matter how many playbooks you write, there's one major challenge to standardization that every company faces: people.

It is impossible to standardize people. Any business where the people are the process, such as consulting and content firms, retainer-based doctor's offices, and law firms, faces this issue. And variations in processes are inherent in any business with a creative component or that tailors their offerings to clients' needs. Usually, people-as-process companies initially succeed due to their founders' unique talents. A key part of that talent is often adaptability. They know when to give clients more or less time and attention, and they might deploy ad hoc processes and payment structures. Because they innately know what to do, they never develop a playbook; they just feel their way through every situation. But when they expand, few (if any) of the new hires possess the same talent as the founder. In these cases, expansion usually engenders a precipitous drop in quality. Thus, the playbooks for the expert talent-driven companies require special care.

The goal should be to strike a balance—provide enough guidance to ensure quality and keep everyone aligned with enough freedom for people to bring their individual genius to work. I've found the best way to achieve this is by standardizing results instead of processes. That's how we handle our playbooks for our dentists. We standardize by requiring three main outcomes: they finish their work in a certain timeframe, they do their work well, and their patients feel comfortable and cared for. As long as they do those three things, we don't need to micromanage or interfere in the process.

A highly successful example of this is McKinsey and Company, the world's foremost management consultancy. McKinsey has an unusually broad mission statement:

> To help our clients make distinctive, lasting, and substantial improvements in their performance and to build a great firm that attracts, develops, excites, and retains exceptional people.

This statement shatters every bit of conventional business wisdom. They don't narrow their market at all. They claim to be able to tackle any problem for any client in any industry. They're trying to be everything to everyone and are possibly the only company in history to accomplish that goal.

They pull this off because of their unique structure and processes. I don't have intimate access to their playbooks, but I know they hire consultants with a wide range of backgrounds. They empower this diverse crew of experts to pursue their unique interests, and even let them turn down any assignment for any reason. The one trait every consultant (and partner) shares is a single-minded dedication to their customers no matter the cost. They all have exceptionally high performance standards. This balance between freedom and accountability is what has allowed the company to reach its ubiquitous status, consulting for national governments, almost every Fortune 500 company, and thousands of other organizations.

It will take creativity, patience, and discipline, but it's possible to create a framework and a set of playbooks that allows any company to scale and thrive. Once you have that, there's no limit to what you'll be able to accomplish.

CHAPTER

SEVEN

Scale It Part 2: Midstage to Maturity

In chapter six we covered a company's journey from infancy to adolescence. Here, we will cover adolescence to middle age. Your baby's high school and college years occur here. This period gets a bit wild. Your company will grow faster than you could ever comprehend, require more resources, and achieve more than you ever thought possible. It will become more independent, and you will have to learn to trust (but verify!) that everything is happening as it's supposed to. Your company will realize the enormity of opportunity that the world offers and will require discipline from you to keep it following the correct path.

If you do it right, this period will bring your business to true maturity, to the absolute prime of its life. You'll be astounded by what your baby has grown to achieve, by the way it helps people live their best lives. To ensure you reach that point, focus on these four keys to success: hire an executive team, evolve into a CEO, maintain connection to the frontlines, and strategize for the future. Let's take a look at each one.

HIRE AN EXECUTIVE TEAM

In previous stages, the founder can wear a few hats (CEO, chief marketing officer, chief operations officer, salesperson). But that becomes impossible during the period of getting a business from high school to maturity. The workforce will expand exponentially during this time, and the company will face challenges that the founder could never have imagined and likely has zero experience in handling. The founder will need help setting strategy and managing growth, so they must choose an exceptional executive team. At this point in Ideal Dental, I followed two rules when hiring executives: prioritize industry-specific expertise and hire people to address future needs.

In practical terms this meant I looked for people who had experience overseeing more retail health locations than we currently had. Of course, it's unrealistic to expect a CMO from a larger company to take an equivalent role at a smaller one. For that reason, we targeted directors and vice presidents who oversee more locations than we currently have. For example, we recruited our CMO, Mike Murphy, from VCA Animal Hospitals, a national veterinary chain. As a director at VCA, Mike oversaw digital marketing for eight hundred locations. When we brought him in, we only had about eighty locations. So even though Mike had never been the top dog in a marketing department, we assumed, correctly, that he'd be able to handle our eighty locations and propel us to eight hundred and beyond. It's like buying clothes for a kid's first day of school. You don't buy an outfit that fits perfectly because in two months the kid outgrows it. Instead, you get the next size or two up so their spiffy new polos and Paw Patrol tees last.

Once you have an excellent executive team, you can step fully into the most important role: that of CEO.

EVOLVE INTO A CEO

Up until now you've been a founder. Unless you work in a specialized industry where your particular expertise is at a premium, you'll need to transition into being a full-time CEO. That means you don't work in the business at all. You don't personally scout locations, you don't devise new marketing strategies, you don't practice your primary craft. At this point your job is to lead, to point the company in the right direction and coordinate the action that propels you forward. And, oh, what a job that is!

When I stepped into my role as CEO, I became busier than I'd ever imagined possible. I felt like I stood in the middle of a large, swirling, delicate machine, and if I stopped pressing all the right buttons, the whole thing would grind to a halt. I quickly learned that in this reality, my first priority had to be to protect my time. This one deserves a closer look.

Protect Your Time

As the CEO time becomes your most precious commodity, so you need to spend it wisely. There are two time-protection mechanisms I rely on the most: organizational charts and minimal meetings.

Organizational Charts

Organizational charts document everyone's roles and responsibilities, as well as to whom they report. This streamlines operations for the entire company. For example, if a regional manager notices there aren't enough new customers per office in their area, they can consult the organizational chart and know exactly which vice president of marketing to approach with the problem. The VP then develops an approach to attract new customers. When everyone follows the organizational chart, it ensures that only the most important and challenging problems reach the CEO, so my time is only required when the issue reaches my level of the organizational chart, which is at the top.

Minimal Meetings

In my experience, people often use meetings to convince themselves they're busy. They spend time setting up the meeting, preparing a PowerPoint presentation, presenting, talking, and following up. This is all fine as long as the meetings accomplish something. But I have to agree with the popular gripe of office workers everywhere: most meetings could have been an email. I only hold meetings that are 100 percent necessary, and usually when people ask me for a meeting, I handle whatever they need with a text or phone call.

Each Monday, I go to a few internal meetings, which I use to check the company's pulse. The first one is always the executive team recap. During these meetings, my top leaders update me on what happened the previous week. Together we review our top line metrics. We look at whether we are expanding too fast (not enough clients per office), or not fast enough (too many clients per office). Then we review in-progress projects, including new location openings, and everyone gives a status update. In the meeting's last block, executives bring up any issues they've encountered. If a market is underperforming or if we saw a sudden drop in customers somewhere, then the team brings it to my attention. I spend the rest of the day meeting with my investors or any other managers who requested extra time with me.

Usually by the end of Monday, I have several tasks to deal with during the rest of the week. I then schedule my week based on the outcomes of these Monday meetings in such a way that allows me to address the most important concerns first. For the most part, those concerns require me to do one of two things: support my staff or develop more efficient processes.

Support the Staff

When my executives raise a particularly thorny problem, I get involved to see how I can help. However, even on these occasions I try not to get too hands-on. I don't tell people how to do their jobs or take over a process. That's not support; that's handling someone else's responsibilities. If I were to make a habit of that, I would train my employees not to take initiative but rather to depend on me and chronically underperform. Instead, I mostly work as a coordinator. I put people in touch with the people they need to fix the issue, or I develop high-level solutions that only I can see or have the authority to approve. Often I do both.

For example, in 2022 during the height of a labor shortage, I asked a regional director during a Monday meeting how their next couple of weeks looked. The director mentioned that some of their offices in Houston faced a severe dental assistant shortage, and that we might have to run below capacity for a while. We were already understaffed, but in Houston, a combination of overlapping illnesses and vacation time requests made those challenges more pronounced. I had been developing a long-term fix to the problem—our own accredited dental assistant training that would double as a talent pipeline and secondary revenue source. But that was years away from fruition. We had yet to find instructors, make sure we didn't break monopoly laws, find locations, develop a curriculum, market it, and wait for a class to graduate. We had also initiated an interim plan to invest heavily in new assistants we had recruited. But none of that would help the office in the immediate weeks.

I asked if they had tried to hire temporary dental assistants. They had, only to discover a tapped pool of temp talent. So I suggested we ask dental assistants on our staff in markets with a labor surplus to see if any would travel to Houston to plug the gaps. I told the regional director to message our regional directors. One of our operations vice presidents passed her request along to offices around the country. We offered assistants willing to travel airfare, meals, a nice hotel, and double their hourly rate. In less than an hour, we had filled all the spots.

This cost a lot, but it was the only way to maintain our volume without sacrificing the customer experience. We likely could have scraped the bottom of the temp barrel and found enough people to keep working, but anyone we brought in wouldn't have understood our processes or felt any sense of loyalty toward Ideal Dental. Using temps would have almost definitely slowed down our operations and likely would have hurt customer satisfaction too. Every day we make a commitment to our customers. If it costs a bit more to keep that promise, then we will pay what it takes, and so should you.

Develop More Efficient Processes

Companies become more complex as they grow. Larger companies generate more data, employ more people, and decision-making power becomes more diffuse. All of this complexity can erode efficiency and prevent employees from quickly addressing challenges or making improvements. A company loses agility when the frontline employees feel they need to run new ideas by managers, those managers feel they need to check with executives, and executives are too far from the frontlines to ever hear about it. Conversely, any new initiative from an executive needs to be disseminated and adopted throughout the company, a process that becomes exponentially more difficult with more people involved.

In 2022, I realized our growth had diminished our agility. To get us back to peak performance, I trained my employees in two methodologies. I call the first Dr. A's Five Rules to Get Shit Done.

1. **Define the Objective and Main Challenges:** To start a trip, you need to have a destination. All around the world people waste countless hours every day on meandering, pointless work. I tell all my employees to prioritize important tasks and clearly define what they hope to accomplish with any actions.
2. **Keep It Simple:** The simpler the solution, the easier it is to implement, and the more likely it is to succeed. I tell my direct reports they should be able to explain any idea they have in less than a minute in simple enough language that a five-year-old would understand. Whenever a team member presents a plan in a meeting, I often have them draw it as a flow chart on the whiteboard. That way I can see how many steps it has and quickly identify spots where we can reduce complexity. For example, if we are rolling out a new ad campaign and I see several hand-offs between the content creation and the website design team in the flow chart, the team member and I can have a conversation about how many of those we actually need and then streamline the process.
3. **Create a measurable plan:** Defining an objective and finding a solution is only half the battle. The key is implementation, so I train my employees to develop a clear plan for how they will implement that solution. A lot of great ideas and initiatives fizzle out because of poor (or nonexistent) planning. An effective plan has clear, simple steps, a timeline, and markers of success. For example, if one of my team members decides to roll out a new scheduling software, then I would like to know when they expect to have the employees trained, when they will make the shift, if they will make it company-wide or phase it in region by region, and how they intend to measure success. Are we successful when every store uses the new system? Or when every store uses it to

shave seconds and minutes off each customer interaction, reduce wait times, and prevent scheduling errors?

4. **Do It**: This is simple. Do what you say you will. All too often, great planners come up with beautiful ideas they never put into practice.
5. **Hold Teams Accountable:** This is where most leaders fail. I've seen it countless times: someone develops a great new system, trains the employees, and it only lasts a month. Good leaders verify that each employee is following through and giving their best effort.

I first presented these rules to my executive team. Once they had internalized the lessons, I noticed a substantial improvement in our workflow. People identified and resolved problems faster. They had greater focus on the important work that made an impact. I also know that most of them passed the rules on to their own direct reports.

I remind my employees that a great way to find places to improve efficiency and reduce complexity is to periodically ask about all processes (especially ones that feel tedious): Why do we do it like this? If the answer has to do with customer needs, then the process may be justified. For example, having every dentist make a follow-up call to the patients they numbed reduces efficiency. But we do it because it enhances the customer experience and makes us unique. If we sacrificed our level of care at the altar of efficiency, our business would suffer.

On the other hand, if you ask that question and can only come up with something like, "Because that's how we've always done it," it's likely there's a more efficient system waiting to be developed. For example, in the mid-2010s I realized we had hired a small army to follow up with insurance companies for reimbursements. The amount of money we spent on this felt excessive, so I investigated. I asked some of the employees how they did their jobs. Apparently, every day they each got an alphabetized list of customer claims to follow up on. Each day, they went down the list, calling the insurance company for each patient. Because we organized the list by customer name, our representatives would call four or five different insurance companies an hour. Often, they would call the same company several times a day. Each time they called, they had to wait on hold for an insurance rep, introduce themselves, and then wait while the rep brought up our file.

When I asked why we did it this way, I heard, "Because that's how I was told to do it."

A huge red flag.

We started to organize patients by insurance provider first and then by last name. This one change saved countless labor hours because now our reps could call each agency once to follow up on multiple claims

It seems so simple and so obvious, but this example underscores an important lesson: often the most brilliant solution is the simplest.

MAINTAIN CONNECTION TO THE FRONTLINES

A large company has innumerable strengths. It reduces costs per unit and generates more revenue, which can be reinvested. It leads to brand recognition that further propels growth and attracts top talent, and it can make a greater positive impact on the world. But growth also comes with the potential for weakness to develop. In general, larger companies are less adaptable than smaller, more agile companies. This is because everyone from the founder all the way down has close, intimate contact with the customer. They know what a customer wants and because they don't have the legacy operations and large bureaucratic mechanisms that larger, more established companies tend to have, the smaller companies can quickly alter their operations to ensure they consistently deliver what the customer needs.

As you grow, you need to do everything you can to maintain start-up-level agility. I do that by visiting as many offices as possible. I used to visit each store as it opened, but that's no longer possible. Instead, I make sure to visit stores whenever I travel for business, and I build time into my schedule to facilitate this. Because I want to get an accurate idea of how each store performs, I don't make a big deal about these visits. In fact, I rarely even give the office notice. I drop in, introduce myself, and observe a bit. If some of our staff are rude, or if one of the doctors takes too long to meet with a patient or finish a procedure, I notice right away. I might observe a couple of appointments and listen to how a staff member handles a few phone calls. I will pull a couple of patient files, look at the X-rays, the diagnoses, and the images to make sure the doctors are doing their work well.

Once I get a sense of how the office operates, I like to chat with the employees when they have free time. I keep the conversations informal because I've found that people are more honest when they feel comfortable. If I were to go in there with a clipboard, inspect every corner of the office, run my finger over the computer monitors to check for dust, and call each employee into a meeting to grill them about their performance and their teammates, they wouldn't trust me. I wouldn't be building a relationship, and I doubt I would hear the truth. Instead, I explain to the employees that my job is to remove as many obstacles from their work as possible. I ask open-ended questions like, "How do you feel about the office in general? Has anything changed recently? Gotten worse? Gotten better? What, if anything, are you struggling with in your role right now?"

Often, the feedback I receive is insightful. Hygienists tell me that old doctors used to perform much better than new doctors, receptionists tell me they haven't been getting as many calls and new guests as usual. Sometimes they will even tell me if they think an office manager isn't doing a good job or is rude to guests and workers. Then I go back and I tell the relevant people (VP ops, director of marketing) to look into the concerns that were raised and make sure we nip any problems in the bud and continue to deliver our best standard of service.

This also helps to motivate the frontline employees. They get to build a relationship with me, and they see how much I care about helping people get out of pain. It humanizes our leadership team and makes them feel like they're an important part of a caring start-up, not a faceless megacorp.

Leverage Frontline Knowledge

A staggering number of companies become enamored with their processes and strictly enforce them. Worse, some companies punish mistakes or missteps so severely that none of their employees feel comfortable enough to take a risk. I take the opposite approach. Every year I kick off our company conference with a speech. And each year I remind all my employees that I consider each of them to be a Picasso. They're creative masters. I remind them that all I want them to focus on is painting. I will handle the rest. I'll provide the canvas and paints and even some creative limits, but I will leave the actual work up to them. The reason for this philosophy is simple: By tapping into the creativity of each employee, we also tap into their knowledge. And because they interact with the customers, they have the most valuable knowledge of all. Just by doing their jobs they learn innately how to solve the three big customer concerns I described at the very beginning: time, money, and fear. More often than not, the frontline workers dream up more elegant solutions than anything I could develop myself.

In practical terms this means I want every employee doing whatever they can to create the best guest experience and most efficient processes, even if that means going a bit against the playbook. Like I said, I impose limits: they can't give away free dental care, offer too many discounts, or increase prices. Other than that, they have free rein to explore new strategies.

Of course it's not enough to simply say I want people to paint masterpieces. I go out of my way to celebrate any new ideas employees come up with, often by directly recognizing those employees at the annual conference and then adding their new improvements to the company's playbooks. While this practice has yielded several improvements, I will focus on two of the most significant contributions.

1. People who don't know about us often assume they won't find a dentist open on Saturdays, so when they have a weekend dental emergency, they go to urgent care or a hospital, where they see a doctor who doesn't understand teeth and can do little more than prescribe pain medication. One of our dentists working in Corinth, a suburb of Dallas, realized we could attract guests by partnering with nearby urgent care centers and hospitals. They called the neighboring health centers to tell those providers we are always open on Saturdays. Since we're designed to accommodate walk-ins, we encouraged those doctors to refer any dental emergencies to us. It was a win-win idea—urgent care centers and emergency rooms would be kept clear of patients they couldn't really help, and the patients would get the treatment they needed faster, and, of course, it brought in more new guests for us.
2. In 2022, one of my regional directors told me about an office they oversaw that had struggled with a string of cancellations. Each cancellation disrupted their carefully calibrated scheduling system and hurt their revenue. Eventually, the office manager told a guest she would gladly change their appointment, but we required a $50 nonrefundable deposit on the new appointment. Suddenly, the guest found a way to keep their original appointment time. The manager told the rest of the front of office staff to impose the same policy. The number of guests who rescheduled dropped

dramatically. The people who actually needed to reschedule still did, and most of them made their rescheduled appointments and didn't lose their deposit. It increased our volume and kept our dentists busy without inspiring complaints. We've adopted this procedure company-wide, and now when people want to reschedule at the last minute, we require a deposit on the new appointment.

In both cases, these employees took initiative and found new and better processes. Granted, the second example was a far bigger risk than the first. Because we'd never posted a deposit policy, the guest might have felt blindsided, especially if they had rescheduled before. Luckily, they seemed to understand the logic, and we didn't get any negative feedback about the policy.

Even if the $50 deposit had flopped, I wouldn't have punished the employee responsible. Creativity requires taking risks. Sometimes those risks backfire. We are lucky enough to be in a position where we can afford to try out new ideas and abandon them if they don't work. If the leadership were to make a negative example of someone who tried something new and experienced a failure, minor or major, while trying to follow my instructions to create their own masterpiece, it would tank morale and kill creativity. Instead, we reward employees for trying new things, even if they don't always work out. As I always say—if you're 75 percent sure you're making the right decision, then follow through. You can always adjust if need be.

STRATEGIZE FOR THE FUTURE

Once your company has achieved maturity, the next step is to keep building on your success. Now is when you can rapidly expand, move to capture market share, and even move into parallel industries. You will have all sorts of momentum, and the worst thing you can do is put unnecessary roadblocks in your path. Speed matters here—once you achieve a degree of success, a host of copycats will spring up. You want to secure a dominant position before they can pose a serious threat. To make sure you do that, I recommend two things: select the correct new markets and evolve without sacrificing your core competency.

Select the Correct New Markets

In this period, you will almost definitely outgrow your original market. For example, at Ideal we went from opening seven or eight locations at a time to opening twenty-five to thirty locations at a time. If we opened thirty or forty locations in one, or even two or three, cities, then we would run the risk of saturating the market and cannibalizing our own business. So we had to create a process to find a steady selection of new markets to move into.

To do that, we built another regression model—this time one that tracked the relationship between average location revenue in a city to several independent variables, most notably median income, total population, rate of population growth, and whether the population was getting younger or older. We found that our stores performed better in higher income cities that were growing and getting younger. For example, Austin emerged as a prime candidate because several companies had lured a lot of young, highly skilled workers to staff their new offices. And those workers were coupling up to start families.

On the other hand, our model steered us away from a place like Daytona Beach, Florida. Daytona Beach has a high median income and a growing population, but it's because so many retirees move there every year, many of whom keep a pied-à-terre in their northeastern hometowns, where they still go for medical care.

Of course, once you select a new market, you have to decide how to enter the new market. Naturally, for a remote or hybrid business, entering new markets is a bit different. If you conduct all your sales and operations digitally, like a software company, then the best way to discover new customers and markets is probably to work with an expert digital marketing agency that can help you get your content in front of the right buyers. If you're a hybrid company, like a consulting firm that does some in-person work as well as remote reviews, then you need to look for low-cost ways to get a physical presence in a new location. You could hire a couple of consultants who have connections in the new city and let them operate from home until you have enough momentum to open an office. Or you could seek out existing consultancies in a city that you can partner with. Maybe you're an excellent culture transformation firm that struggles with operations-based consulting. You could reach out to operations companies about jointly creating programs in a specific area and market them to local organizations. Either way, both models are much easier, less costly, and less risky than a brick-and-mortar expansion.

Land and Expand

Whenever we enter a new market, we follow the same strategy, which I call land and expand. It is the polar opposite of a soft launch. We aim to make a splash by opening several (at least eight, if not more) offices at once or in close succession. By doing so, we get two main benefits. For one, it helps us quickly build momentum. If we have an office in several parts of the city, we can blanket the entire area in advertisements and capture a lot of attention. In essence, it allows us to get more bang for each advertising buck because someone might see an ad for us in the neighborhood where they work, get curious, look us up, and discover that we also have a location where they live.

Second, landing and expanding in one town is much cheaper than opening one office in eight different cities. For each new city, we need to establish a new regional hub with a regional manager and a building team dedicated to handling the local legal requirements. Because each hub requires so much specialized labor, it takes roughly the same number of employees to run a regional hub that covers eight offices as it does to manage one. More hubs, more expenses.

I've explained how we like to build our offices from scratch because it lets us create the exact culture we want. While this is true, there are times when acquisitions make more sense, like when you're trying to break into a new market. For example, when we expanded into Houston, the first city we entered outside of the Dallas-Fort Worth area, we knew we wanted to open eight new offices at once. We didn't have any investment capital, so we had to go into debt to fund them all. We needed to mitigate this sizeable risk, so I decided on taking the acquisitions route because buying an office would grant us access to a patient list. That way we could ensure some revenue while our new offices got their footing. We ended up building four offices, buying four, and then building four more in Houston before the year was over.

We evaluated potential acquisitions according to three main factors: profitability, location, and culture. The entire point of this strategy was to guarantee income, so obviously we needed each office to turn a profit. Location, of course, determines profitability, and we used our location regression model to estimate future revenue for each option. We also looked into what sort of building the offices occupied.

I'd estimate that about 80 percent of dentist offices are completely unidentifiable from the street. They're usually on the third floor of an office building that's part of a block of identical office buildings thirty minutes away from the city center, and their only sign is a placard on the building directory. We wanted to be near the street in a welcoming commercial development where we could put up our customary hyper-visible signage. Since we were new to that city, we needed people to know we were there.

Finally, we made sure that each office's culture, somewhat easily blended in with ours. We didn't want to dilute our brand, but we also didn't want to alienate the client list by letting go of all the employees currently working in the office. So we observed how each office's staff worked and only bought the ones that demonstrated our commitment to service.

The last part of my land-and-expand strategy is to never back away from a fight. I believe if you have identified the right gaps in the market, you will win against any competition you find yourself facing. So when entering a new market, we look for direct competitors (multi-office dental brands) and open a few offices near their locations.

In late 2019, Ideal Dental decided to move into the Orlando market, where there were already three huge players in retail dental. Other owners might have chosen to stay out of Orlando entirely, thinking that the market would be too hard to break into. But when we did our research, we realized we had certain key advantages over our two main competitors: we were open more days, and we didn't refer our guests to outside specialists. That, and after we read through some of their online reviews, we realized they struggled to have consistently excellent customer service and even struggled a bit clinically. Because we had that edge, I knew we could carve market share away from them, especially because I trusted that our dentistry would also ultimately prove to be of better quality than theirs.

When we were exploring opening our first store in Orlando, our locations team drew up a list of potential spots. One of the locations was perfect: it was in an affluent neighborhood, which meant it would be close to a lot of people in our target demographic. There was only one problem: that location was so good that two of our major retail competitors were already there. When I saw that, I knew it was exactly the spot to open our first office. Some people on my team thought it might be easier for us to find a foothold in a different part of the city before we expanded into territory saturated by our competitors. But I was confident in our ability to stand out, to take these other offices head-on and win. I knew we had the best in-house dental training, I knew we offered the best convenience, and I knew we took care of our guests from start to finish in a way our competitors didn't.

I wanted to announce our presence in the new city, to let the other companies know we were there to compete with them and to send a message to my staff that we were there to beat out these other two retail chains. I think it helped to keep everyone focused and to funnel the top talent in the city toward us. We started to see dentists who worked for our competitors take interest in what we did, and some of them even applied for jobs with us. As young dentists looking for their first jobs saw us right next to the two major competitors, it positioned us as a competitive player even though some of these companies were bigger than us.

It worked. Within a couple of years, we dominated that market.

Overall, the transition from mid-stage to full maturity is a period of unprecedented growth. After our second finance deal, Ideal Dental was opening about thirty to forty stores a year. But something was happening that hadn't since the very early days, before I had figured out the playbooks: not all of those stores were performing exactly as I expected. Some of the underperformers eventually succeeded, but many of them failed.

This haunted me. We had never had to shutter an office before, and I felt like a failure. I was also still dogged, as I am today, by the sense that at any moment everything I built could disappear. What if the closed stores were portents of trouble to come? I obsessed about this, had the team get back into the guts of our location-opening regression model, and consider retooling our advertising strategy.

By this time, I had become friends with Nigel Travis, who during his time as the CEO of Dunkin' Brands, from 2009 to 2018, opened over six thousand new stores.[1] I mentioned to him my frustration with how many of my new offices weren't making the cut. He gave some incredible advice that helped give me perspective and kept me from doing anything drastic to solve a perceived issue. He told me that when you're opening locations at the clip I was, about 10 percent of them won't work. And that's OK. It's not a sign of decay or of a major problem that requires fixing. This calmed me down. I had somewhat suspected it, but hearing it from someone who had already been in my position made the message much more powerful.

Seek Partnerships and Synergies

When your company becomes a national brand, it gives you a special allure. It gives you a certain heft that makes almost every part of your operations less expensive. You can negotiate bulk prices from vendors, better lease rates, better advertising rates. You attract better talent because most top performers want to work with the top dog. You can also leverage this new recognition to find interesting ways to partner with other national brands, potentially opening new frontiers for investment and advertising, and to lower costs.

For example, one of my good friends happens to own Smoothie King, a national chain of quick-service restaurants specializing in smoothies and smoothie bowls. Around since the 1970s, Smoothie King has used the increased American demand for healthy quick-service restaurants to rapidly expand in the twenty-first century. For years before I met this man, Smoothie King had been one of the businesses we opened our own locations near because we share a common ideal customer. We've since developed a few cross-promotions—people receive a free smoothie after visiting us for the first time, and people can receive a free teeth-whitening session with a smoothie purchase.

We also started to collaborate on real estate in two important ways. We began to hunt for retail spaces to lease together because it would give us greater negotiating power with a landlord. Most landlords want to fill their spaces as quickly as possible. If we approach them and say that two national brands are willing to move in immediately but at a slightly lower rate than the asking price, they usually rent to us, especially because our high-traffic businesses will make any other vacant part of the retail lot more desirable. A company like Chipotle or Panera Bread or McDonald's or Whole Foods might see we're set up in the same area and decide to lease a space nearby. Together, our two brands spawn a mini economic ecosystem and help solve most landlords' number one problem: a lack of reliable tenants.

Evolve Without Sacrificing Your Core Competency

Larger companies face a surfeit of options. As the management team grows, more people will bring fresh perspectives and ideas. While this is a benefit, it also makes it easier to get distracted from the core competency. For a somewhat controversial and high-profile example of this, look at Elon Musk. Despite owning a sliver of the market share compared to legacy automakers, he managed to build Tesla into one of the most valuable car manufacturers in the world. Then he bought Twitter, and Tesla's valuation tanked. He strayed from his core competency and paid the price. Of course, danger lurks at the other extreme as well. A static company is in many ways a dying one. (For more on this, see the now cliché stories about Kodak, Blockbuster, and the like.)

The goal should be to evolve in a way that furthers your grand vision and core values. Even if you believe you can win more customers, you should never go off-brand to do it. For example, in about 2008, Texas increased the reimbursement rate that the state Medicaid paid dentists.

One of my early partners suggested that if we opened offices in areas with a lot of Medicaid recipients, we could probably turn a profit. I decided against it. We would have to control costs by building lower-quality offices and paying our dentists less. It would dilute our brand. We became successful by targeting a specific customer, and we had not even come close to fully tapping that initial market.

We didn't need to significantly overhaul our model to fulfill our mission, but there are countless companies that have to great effect. A perfect example of this is Netflix. According to the standard narrative, Netflix shouldered out Blockbuster (I know, cliché, but bear with me) because DVD deliveries were more convenient than brick-and-mortar stores, but that's only a small part of the story. Netflix had set out to provide a better, more enjoyable customer experience overall. DVD delivery was merely a sliver of that. They also eliminated late fees, a decision that drove the exodus from Blockbuster more than anything else. Then when technology advanced to make streaming possible, Netflix seized that opportunity. It seemed like an abrupt shift because they abandoned the original business plan (DVD delivery, no late fees) that had given them a foothold. But in reality it was merely a superficial change because they sustained and improved upon the core competency (a convenient, pleasant customer experience) that had underpinned their success.

SCALING BEYOND THE CORE COMPETENCY

Eventually, if you work hard and smart, you create your own luck, and you will be in a position to scale beyond your core competency. It's impossible to say exactly when you should start thinking about that, but a good rule of thumb is to wait until you reach a point where your core business can continue to expand and maintain itself with minimal direct oversight, and it generates enough revenue to fund its growth and subsidize other pursuits. Another good way to tell is if you've already essentially expanded to the limits of your core competency.

For example, Starbucks started as a coffee shop. Then they started to add other items such as baked goods, premade sandwiches, cold drinks, and coffee accessories. Now they're selling protein packs. They've expanded, but they did so within the realm of a café. We did the same at Ideal by gradually adding more hours and more specialists to existing locations. Once we accomplished this, I decided it was time to expand. But keep in mind that how you decide to expand matters. To get the most out of new ventures, protect your core competency and expand strategically.

Protect Your Core Competency

Protecting your core competency is simple—keep your various operations distinct from one another. At the very least, create new divisions within the company. More often, however, protecting your core competency requires creating a new company or subsidiary. This will prevent your core competency from being diluted by the other competing forces in the new division.

For example, my first major expansion beyond Ideal Dental was my oral care line, ToothScience. I decided to make ToothScience its own company with its own board and a CEO other than me because it was completely different from what Ideal Dental does. A dental product manufacturer has dramatically different needs than a dental brand. They need to focus on such processes as complying with FDA and state regulations, sourcing materials, manufacturing products, and developing a distribution network. The marketing strategy for a consumer product line is also completely different from a consumer service brand.

Expand Strategically

When moving beyond your core competency, try to first move into markets that overlap with your original purpose so you're not starting from scratch. You can leverage your preexisting expertise and connections to quickly grow and succeed. This can help reinforce your original business's industry foothold as well—a large part of why I expanded into an oral care line in the first place. I was a clinician, as were many of my trusted colleagues. Years of direct experience with my clients' teeth, and even more time spent reviewing academic journals and research, had taught me exactly what to look for in a product line that would enhance patients' oral care and systemic health.

In short, I could leverage my expertise. I could choose materials I knew led to a healthier, brighter smile for all my patients and our future customers. Expanding also allowed me to directly own a much greater share of the dental care market overall while taking advantage of obvious synergies between the two businesses. Every year we treat more than one million patients. They have relationships with our dentists. They trust us. They know we put a premium on clinical results and patient safety. When we developed a top-quality dental care line, we had a ready-made customer base.

This is the same process that several of the largest and most successful companies in the world have followed. For example, Google's core competency was helping people find exactly what they want. They developed advanced algorithms that predicted human behavior and the capacity to store and sort unfathomable amounts of data. This gave them an obvious, and lucrative, avenue for expansion: they could leverage this technology and expertise to sell ads that could target customers with profound specificity.

Some companies stray almost willy-nilly from their original core purpose. In the short term this sometimes works to boost profits and generate shareholder value. However, in the long term this approach usually erodes whatever made the company great, leaving it without a solid foundation to stand on and sometimes bringing it to the brink of financial ruin. A perfect example of this is General Electric under Jack Welch. Before Welch, General Electric made most of their money from manufacturing. Thanks to Welch's leadership, the company grew rapidly, but they completely transformed. They developed a robust financial arm and bought a controlling stake in NBC, among other companies. The manufacturing fell by the wayside. The quality of their products dipped, and they ceded swaths of market share in their field. The company's valuation jumped by over $400 billion, but it was unsustainable. As soon as Welch left, the company ended up worse off than they were before.[2]

CHAPTER

EIGHT

Fund Your Growth

By now you've built a company that's like a beautiful souped-all-the-way-up Ferrari Monza SP1 V12 with 799 wild-eyed froth-mouthed horses straining at the bridle. Forget about rubber, this will burn the asphalt. We're talking power, so much speed that it might just take off and fly. You have all this potential to charge toward the future and unleash the power, but you need the highest-quality fuel, and lots of it.

For a company, that fuel is capital. And at this point, loans from banks will not cut it. The loans are like regular unleaded: easy to access but heavy. Too much in a nice car will gunk up the engine. You need to burn clean and use the superpremium stuff. That comes in the form of investment capital. Instead of taking on more debt and more risk, you can sell a part of your company for a cash transfusion, which you can use to ensure your family's financial future and to kick your company into the next gear.

But the capital-raising process is a whole new world. It has its own language, opportunities, and challenges. In this chapter, I will map out the world for you and give advice on how to best navigate it. I start with my golden rule: the best time to sell is when you don't have to.

WHEN TO SELL ALL OR PART OF YOUR BUSINESS

When to sell a stake in your company to investors is one of the most important business decisions you will make. And just as it is true with so many opportunities, timing is everything. I follow two essential rules to ensure I make a deal with equity investors at the perfect time: don't sell too early and sell from a position of strength.

Don't Sell Too Early

In 2005, Alexis Ohanian and Steve Huffman, two students at the University of Virginia, founded a new online social media platform called Reddit. At the time, Ohanian was twenty-two years old. They completed the site and rolled it out within sixteen months. Their user base grew exponentially, as did ad revenue. And best of all, with only four employees, the organization had minimal overhead. Condé Nast, the global mass media company that publishes, among other things, *The New Yorker* and *Vanity Fair* magazines, approached Ohanian and Huffman. They offered to buy Reddit for $10 million. The founders eagerly agreed. As of 2022, Reddit was valued at more than $3 billion.

The youthful founders made a common and costly mistake. They didn't think through why they were selling. They saw the most money anyone had ever put in front of them and took it. Better to view selling (all or part) of your business as a tool to help you achieve specific goals, not as an escape hatch. The only reason I've sold part of my company was to raise the capital I needed to expand faster than I could before. I didn't even consider taking on investors until I grew the company as much as I could by leveraging debt. The first time I went through a fundraising round, where I agreed to sell a portion of my company for capital, I had thirty locations, all running smoothly. We could only open seven offices a year with banks, and I wanted to open at least twenty a year. I didn't need the money from the sale to improve my lifestyle. I didn't plan on leaving the business. I just wanted to create a larger impact, and investors made that possible for me.

Sell from a Position of Strength

Savvy investors constantly search for the best possible deals. Often, they look for what's called a distressed asset, a business that might have sound fundamentals or obvious potential but faces some steep, immediate challenges. This is the finance version of buy low, sell high. Since every business goes through rough spots, often outside of the founder's control, you will likely face a situation where someone tries to buy you low, but you must sell high.

For example, in early 2020 I realized we had outgrown our original finance partners. We wanted to open about forty offices a year, and our current partners could not fund that. I was thinking about soliciting new investors when COVID-19 hit. The world ground to a halt. We, like everyone else, faced unprecedented uncertainty. The entire nation was under lockdown, and people stopped going to the dentist, even when they legally could, to avoid exposure. This became the worst stretch for our business in years, and would have been an awful time to try to open forty new offices. Therefore, I decided to delay the funding process until we returned to some degree of normalcy.

During that pause, two investment firms expressed interest in Ideal Dental. One happened to be one of the most storied investment companies in the world, so I took a few meetings with them. Without mobilizing the full army of lawyers and accountants, they offered me enough capital to get my attention. I took a string of late-night calls with one of the partners, during which we went through some early negotiations. I noticed a pattern. Each time we talked, they made the offer a little worse. One day they demanded that they'd get paid before all other investors or creditors in the case of our success or bankruptcy. Then they reduced their overall valuation of the company. They blamed this on the uncertainty created by COVID-19, claiming it had made my business a much riskier investment.

Now, if I'd sold at this point, I would have broken my own rule. A small part of me was already wondering if we would make it, and here came these investors offering me a windfall that I could use to protect my family and even keep the business afloat through the uncertainty of an extended pandemic. They clearly wanted to make me think I needed to sell, and it almost worked. We continued to negotiate, and the firm kept lowering their price. I became a little fixated on this deal and told my team that if we could get them to a certain number, we would take it. We never got there. Eventually, they made a final offer, and we rejected it.

This put me in a funk for the next couple of weeks. I had thought our company would be worth way more than what they'd offered. But it turned out to be a huge blessing and a reminder of how important it is to choose the right time to sell.

Shortly after that company backed out, the first COVID-19 vaccines hit the market. The governors of the states where we had most of our offices—Texas and Florida—started to aggressively roll back COVID-19 restrictions. Public perception in those areas changed, people realized that dentists, with our fastidious attention to disinfecting and reducing the spread of contagion, were perhaps among the safest businesses to visit. Our profits skyrocketed as people rushed to make up for the appointments they had missed.

Shortly after that flood of customers, we opened another round of funding. This time we accepted an offer worth $200 million more than the best offer the other firm had made, less than a year after that deal broke down.

NAVIGATE THE FUNDRAISING PROCESS

Once you've a reached a place where you feel like you can sell from a position of strength, you need to actually know how to navigate the fundraising process. There are four keys to a successful sale: show profits, show and sell what's unique, choose the right investors, and leverage investor expertise.

Show Profits

As of 2022, Uber, one of the largest brands in the world, had never posted an annual profit in its thirteen-year history.[1] They were not alone. An incomplete list of well-known but unprofitable companies includes Airbnb, Stripe, Epic Games (makers of the Gen Z sensation Fortnite), Zillow, and Peloton. Each of those companies has existed for at least a decade, and Epic Games has been around for more than thirty years.[2]

Not posting a profit isn't mere financial recklessness but rather a business strategy. These companies use their millions (or billions) in revenue and investment capital to develop new products, such as Rivian did when they developed new electric vehicles, or they sell their goods and services at a loss to cripple competitors and capture market share, such as Amazon did by undercutting other online retailers until Amazon achieved a near monopoly on ecommerce.

Start-ups often do both. That's the path Uber took, funneling large amounts of money into developing their app and algorithms, then offering rides (or food delivery) in as many cities as possible at a price that cab companies couldn't compete with. Once they conquered the market, they raised rates, including exorbitant surge pricing, and cut their overall costs.[3] It worked, sort of. In 2023, they posted a profit for the first time, largely due to their stakes in other companies as they continued to run their ride-hailing and delivery arm at a loss.[4]

This business model crops up most frequently in the tech world, where companies must invest in R and D to get an edge over their stiff competition. That being said, I've seen service companies and manufacturers try to follow this route with less success. For example, in 2022 I met with the founders of a company I was considering buying. They owned a group of about four or five specialized dental offices, and while they showed plenty of revenue, they had no profit. They asked me to value them on a multiple of their revenue, however, not their profit, because they claimed to be reinvesting their revenue in a way that would ensure growth.

Not a chance.

The burn-cash, grow-fast business model is a little bit like a live-fast, die-young lifestyle. Sometimes, as with Mick Jagger, you don't actually die young, and you go on to have a long and successful career. More often, like Jimi Hendrix or Janis Joplin, you burn brilliantly for a while and then you do, in fact, die young. Or maybe you never burn brilliant at all. Only a tiny fraction of companies that go decades without posting a profit ever manage to become profitable. In fact, this strategy was one of the direct causes of the first dot-com bubble and crash.

Part of the reason so many unprofitable companies crash is because they're far more susceptible to outside shocks than their profitable counterparts. Since they rely on a steady stream of capital, as soon as money lending becomes tighter (due to the fed raising interest rates), their money dries up, and the companies' values tank. We saw this play out in 2022 when the fed combatted inflation by pushing up interest rates. The stock market fell in general, but an index of unprofitable tech stocks compiled by Goldman Sachs underperformed the NASDAQ-100 by as much as 35 percent.[5]

It's much smarter to run a lean and profitable company from the start. It not only makes your company more resilient to outside factors, it also dramatically increases the price you can demand during negotiations. For Ideal Dental, we focused on two key profit metrics: our overall profit and our profits per location. We showed investors both because one can fluctuate a lot more than the other. When we go through periods of expansion, hire a lot of new employees, and pay to open several new shops, our overall profit drops because we're spending more without yet showing new revenue. Our per location profit, on the other hand, stays steady. Once an Ideal Dental location reaches maturity, it turns about the same sizeable profit every quarter. That's the number we highlight for potential investors.

Most investors agree with me and value a company based on a multiple of the profit. The higher the profit, the higher the price. More than pure profit, however, investors also want to see historical consistency. Now that I'm doing some investing of my own, I see a lot of companies that in the post-COVID-19 boom economy have turned in wild amounts of profit. They think they're ready to sell for a big number, but I wouldn't be ready to make that sort of an investment. Fads can come and go. Investors need to know the company they're thinking of investing in will stick around.

Show and Sell What's Unique

Beyond profitability in the present day, it's vital that you prove you have a unique approach and well-developed processes that will guarantee future profits for years to come. If you've paid attention to and acted on the first part of this book, then you're most of the way there. So much of what makes a company unique are its grand vision, differentiation from competitors, market niche, and playbooks. The key is knowing how to communicate the value that these differentiators bring and being able to prove it.

For example, during our second funding process, my team and I had a large dinner with the key players from one of the firms that had submitted a bid to buy us. I sat next to one of the firm's partners. We had a lovely evening. We talked a bit about business, a bit about the food, and got to know each other.

My team had a completely different experience. As I was driving home from the restaurant, I had a conference call with my team. Apparently, the representatives from the equity firm had been rude and condescending. They told my team that our analysis was all wrong and our business model didn't work. They warned everyone to look out because in the meeting the next day they were going to grill us and make us realize how misguided our analysis was.

I took this personally. As I've said, I hold and nourish a deep conviction that my company is the best. These people had insulted me, my work, and my team, and I felt the need to protect us.

We were slated to pitch Ideal Dental the next morning. We would present our case and then the equity people would give theirs. Presumably so we'd know what to expect, the equity people had sent us a binder that contained all the reasoning behind their valuation. Even though we had spent weeks preparing for the meeting, I pulled out their binder as soon I returned to my house. I scoured each page and made careful notes so I could challenge each point of their argument.

In a nutshell, they compared our business to a different dental brand they had invested in. They claimed we couldn't sustain our growth because our doctor turnover rate was too high. They cited data from the other dental practice that showed that whenever a doctor left, sales plummeted and took a long time to rebound. The previous dental company had a doctor turnover rate of 1 percent per year. We sometimes would turn over 20 percent of our doctors a year.

In the meeting, we went off script. Instead of going through the presentation we'd rehearsed, I came in and made the argument I had prepared the night before. I explained their argument had one glaring fallacy: they were comparing apples to oranges.

Their old company had been a group of dentist-owned-and-operated offices. Patients developed a direct connection with their personal dentist, not with the brand. Any dentist who left their company took all their patients with them, so of course the sales cratered.

I told them it insulted me to even be compared to the old model. At Ideal, we are a brand, and we inspire loyalty to the brand, not to the individual dentists. We are far more similar to Walgreens. It doesn't matter who the pharmacist behind the counter is, the experience is always the same. In the same way, each of our doctors is an employee, dedicated to delivering the best customer experience. We show higher turnover rates because we have no patience for underperforming doctors. And, as our data showed, our sales improved after a dentist departed one of our offices. Beyond that, our offices continued to grow. My team members chimed in with supporting data and context when needed.

Each of our offices had regularly posted a double-digit growth rate year over year. Their offices? Just 1 percent. So I said, "Okay, we let some doctors go. Your other company doesn't. But maybe they should because when we do it, our offices perform better and grow faster as a result than anything that company or anyone else in the industry does."

After I'd said my piece, a young guy started in with some aggressive questioning about our data and our assumptions. He came across as sneering and condescending. In the middle of his line of questioning, he said something that outright contradicted their own analysis.

I cut him off and told him to flip to the page in his company's booklet with the numbers that contradicted his own point. I knew his analysis better than he did because I'd prepped the entire night before. I kept pointing him to different parts of his analysis and breaking down why it didn't hold up. As we were leaving, one of the investors came over and told my team, "That was the best presentation I have ever seen."

During the debrief, one of my team members told me he wished they had recorded that presentation because we had never spoken as eloquently or as forcefully before. All I had done was lay out exactly what made us unique. The investors loved it and almost immediately called to increase their bid. For weeks after, they kept calling, inviting my team and me to steak dinners, drinks, and shows. They spent millions of dollars on lawyers, bankers, and labor trying to put together more compelling bids and packages so they could stay in the process. It got to the point that the head of the company came to me and said, "Look, this is somewhat embarrassing, but I have to know. Do we even have a chance? What can I do to make this happen?"

In the end, we didn't go with them, but we did keep them in consideration until the final round. And I was able to use their enthusiasm as a bargaining chip to help me negotiate better terms from the company that we ultimately went with. I had shown exactly what made us unique, and they were desperate to work with us.

Choose the Right Investors

You may have gathered this from what you've read already, but just in case you missed it, sophisticated financial partners don't just dole out money and hope the business succeeds. As soon as they invest, they become a business partner. So pick a partner you're excited to work with. To choose the right investor, consider these four factors: operational autonomy, commitment, the deal, and future opportunities.

1. **Operational Autonomy:** Once someone buys a stake in your company, they will exercise at least some control and influence over your operations. I recommend taking the deal that maximizes your autonomy. In my experience, founders know how to run their business better than equity partners because the founders have industry expertise and a more intimate knowledge of their customers' needs. Sometimes when an equity group takes too much control, they make changes that compromise the business's core values and brand promise.

   This happened, for example, to the sports media publication Deadspin. Deadspin's early success came from a unique blend of explosive, well-researched investigative sports journalism and humorous takes on pop culture and sports. This powered a meteoric rise, which led to a string of acquisitions. Eventually, a private equity firm snapped them up, saw that the most profitable part of the site was sports, and ordered the editors to stick to sports. The editors resigned in protest. Since then, Deadspin's readership has fallen by *90 percent*.[6]

   This would be akin to a firm buying a controlling stake in my company, looking at our expenses and operations, and saying, "You know what, we can probably do the same amount of work with one less dentist per office if we book appointments closer together and tell our dentists to work even faster." Or they might say, "Why do we spend so much money training our dentists? Why can't they learn on the job?"

   The result would be that we would no longer offer the best care with the most convenience to the most people. We would become just like all the other retail dental offices. We might post slightly better profits per store simply because the change would lower costs, but we would have sacrificed everything that makes us unique.

I would never let this happen. But I can only prevent such a cataclysmic scenario because I refuse to cede my controlling stake. Your business is your baby. When looking for an investment partner, don't sell them your child. Bring them in as a nice step-parent, someone who will support you but never question whether you know what's best. The one caveat would be unless your partner is pushing back heavily on something that is not the core of your business. If they're insistent about a financial maneuver or something in their wheelhouse, it can make sense to defer. Just do not compromise what made you special in the first place.

2. **Commitment:** How committed will each potential investor be to your success? While it might seem that any investor would be, well, equally invested, commitment levels vary. For example, at a young equity firm, you might be their cornerstone investment. If your company fails, the investor's fails. In that case, the investment managers will probably lavish time, attention, and resources on you. On the other hand, with a larger and more established investment group, you might get lost in the crowd. However, one is not inherently better than the other, and each situation comes with advantages and disadvantages. Extra support usually comes with extra scrutiny, and therefore less operational freedom, and vice versa. If you feel like you need the support and can maintain enough operational control to keep your business's core intact, then by all means partner with a smaller firm. If you feel confident in your ability to oversee rapid growth and want a laissez-faire partner, go with a more established group.

3. **The Deal:** Like snowflakes, each investment offer is unique. Expect potentially hundreds of different conditions and terms to pop up in a deal, which your lawyers and banker can help you understand. What matters most is how much money they offer and what percent of your company they want in return. Remember, these deals are a tool to help grow your company and give you an opportunity to take some chips off the table. In other words, take some of the value of your company as cash, so you're not entirely dependent on the company's continued success for your financial security. Make sure that any deal you take offers enough capital for you to reach your goals without giving up control of your destiny.
4. **Future Opportunities:** The best finance partners fuel success by opening new doors. During the fundraising process, make sure to ask about other companies in their portfolio that you might be able to partner with to find new synergies or about the ways that the firm supports their portfolio companies to reach new heights.

The significance of each of these factors depends on your individual goals. For example, if you want to retire, then you probably care more about getting as much money as possible, and less about operational autonomy. If you want to stay in control of your business, then autonomy will matter more. To better understand how to make these decisions, let's look at two examples: my own and a friend of mine who I will call Todd.

My company went through two funding rounds. The first came in 2015 when I had thirty locations, all turning a profit. I felt secure. The worst struggles—the sleepless nights, the cold morning drives to the bank hoping to cover payroll—were behind me. Numerous investors had been bombarding me with emails and phone calls. They were all "so interested in my business" and wanted to treat me to a steak dinner.

At first I accepted all the invitations. It was fun. They asked all sorts of questions about my business. They waxed poetic about how great they thought my business was and how with their help and funding we could really slam the old pedal to the proverbial metal.

Now remember: I'm a dentist who became a businessman. I never studied finance. At the time I didn't understand equity and acquisitions. These representatives showed up asking stuff like, "What's your EBITDA? What's your four-wall margin? What's your leverage?" And I'd say, "What is EBITDA? What are four-wall margin and leverage?" Because I couldn't follow the conversations, I didn't want to sell. I knew if I continued with this level of ignorance, I would make a huge mistake. Eventually I stopped taking the calls and meetings.

About six months later, an investment banker reached out to me. Now investment bankers, unlike venture capital or private equity firms, don't directly invest. Instead, they help companies raise capital and negotiate deals. Because he wasn't trying to buy my company, and because I thought he could answer my questions, I took the meeting. He started off talking about how strong he thought the business was, then asked, "So, tell me: What is the next step? What do you want to do with the business?"

My first option was to sell the whole company, take my profits, and exit. A lot of people might have taken this route and either retired or moved on to other ventures, as Reddit's Alexis Ohanian did. Sometimes that is the right move. For every Ohanian who sold and watched their former company take off, there are several people who did not sell only to have the company flounder.

My second option was to sell a controlling stake in the company and continue to serve on the board. This happens a lot when companies go through their first funding cycle, often because the potential equity partner believes that the founder is not fit to serve as the CEO.

My third option was to continue with the status quo, taking on more debt and slowly expanding through Texas.

I didn't want any of this. I had just recently had my first child, Daniel, and I didn't want to continue to take on debt that might jeopardize my family's financial future. As it was, I already had several personal guarantees on large loans and leases. If something tragic happened to me, those would get passed on to my family. So I told the banker that I wanted to maintain control of the business, grow faster without taking more risk, and hopefully find enough money to get myself out of those personal guarantees. At that point, we were only opening about seven new locations a year. He asked, "How many locations a year do you want to open, and what's stopping you from doing that?" I told him that I wanted to get to a point where we could open twenty locations at a time, but we couldn't because our banks wouldn't give us enough of a loan.

The investment banker suggested I bring in a finance partner. I balked. I had just been having all these conversations and had already decided I didn't want to sell. Then the banker asked, "How much money would you need to see to consider selling a part of your business?"

I was tired of the entire conversation, so I gave him a number that I hoped was so outrageous it would keep people away.

The banker didn't even blink. He simply asked me to send him some financial information, and he would tell me if it was realistic. Once I did, he called and said, "I think we can get you your number."

We started a fundraising process in which we invited finance firms to submit bids for my company. We comfortably cleared my original number, and by the end I was choosing between two firms, a brand-new one and a more established one. I remember sitting across from the founder of the new firm, looking him in the eyes, and realizing that if I went with him, then he would have everything riding on my company. We would be his first and only major investment. His company had offered slightly less than their more established competitor, but I had a gut feeling that I could trust this man.

That, and I wanted a partner who would view my success as completely connected to theirs. In *The Art of War*, Sun Tzu talks about how soldiers always fight the hardest if they have no option to retreat. If the only way to survive is through victory, they will do whatever they can to win. It's the underlying logic behind the Allies storming the beaches of Normandy, and it's what I wanted in a partnership. I didn't have the chance to retreat, and I didn't want my partners to have that option either.

I went with the younger company, and it worked out. We grew rapidly. Eventually we got large enough that we had the infrastructure, staff, and revenue to open more offices than our current banking partnership could support. So we started a second funding process. This time, we only considered larger, more established firms. We had proven we could turn a profit at scale. I entered the process with a clear goal: to double our size from 85 locations to 170 in the first sixteen months of the partnership and expand nationwide.

In the second round, twelve firms submitted bids, and eventually I narrowed it down to the six that offered the best terms. From there, I narrowed it down to our top three choices by assessing what resources each could offer. At this point I gathered as much information about each firm as I could. I talked to the leaders of companies from each firm's portfolio to see how their investors operated. I asked questions like, "How long have you worked together? Tell me about a challenge you faced and how your partners helped you. Did you face any challenges and not receive the support you needed? Have you had major disagreements? Were there times when something they suggested didn't work out or when you felt you'd lost too much autonomy?" Everyone I spoke to was extremely candid, and I got a sense that just two of the firms would give me the freedom I needed, so I eliminated the third.

I was down to two choices, both with essentially identical offers. I remember calling Todd Hirsch, the representative from Blackstone, one of the two remaining companies. I asked, "Why should we choose you?" He said, "Because I'm here. It's a Sunday, and I'm on a call with you trying to figure this out. I will care as much as you and do whatever I can, work whenever I need to, to make sure we succeed."

That was what I needed to hear. I wanted someone who was committed to me. And he backed it up by how he described their vision of the future. They were ready to help take Ideal Dental national. The other company wanted me to focus on Texas and Florida. When I told Blackstone during negotiations that I had always wanted to create the Starbucks of dentistry, they didn't laugh or act surprised. Instead, the first thing they said was, "Well, we work with the founder of Starbucks. Would you be curious about having him on your board? If so, we can talk to him about it."

So I went with Blackstone. They were perfect—supportive without being overbearing and with unparalleled resources, a sterling track record, and the most expansive network imaginable. In the end, we sent Howard Schultz, the CEO of Starbucks, the information, asking if he wanted to invest or become a board member. Ultimately, he decided it wouldn't make sense because he couldn't add very much value to a dental company. But that didn't matter—I had the opportunity to bring it up with him, and that sort of access is priceless.

Now let's look at my friend Todd, who owns a chain of restaurant and performance venues. I invested in one of his first locations and received an incredible return. Even in the middle of the COVID-19 pandemic, when restaurants and performance venues struggled, Todd brought in $12 million per store per year. Investors noticed his success, made him some offers, and he came to me for advice. At the time he was considering two different proposals. One came from an individual investor, a billionaire who owned one of the largest fast-food franchises in the country. He offered to fund 50 percent of all Todd's future locations as long as Todd wouldn't take on any other investors and make up the other 50 percent with debt. The other offer came from a private equity group in Canada that owned a lot of real estate and sports and performance complexes. They wanted to invest in his company as a private equity partner and help him open locations either in or around some of the complexes they owned.

I explained to my friend that he had three options at this point. He could take either of those deals, find a banker and invite bids from other investors before he made his decision, or continue with the status quo. He had already made so much money that any of his previous investors, including me, would eagerly fund new locations. I told him that from my perspective the worst option was to go with the individual investor. Based on Todd's track record, he wouldn't struggle to find investors, and there was no reason to grant one person exclusive investment rights and take on so much debt. While that investor could theoretically connect him to a lot of successful people in the restaurant industry and serve as a mentor, the risks outweighed the benefits. Worst of all, with that deal, Todd couldn't take any money off the table for himself. All the capital would go straight to opening new locations.

To choose between the remaining three options, we needed to crunch some numbers. I asked for some financial information and put together a rough valuation of his company. In the end, I estimated Todd should make about $30 million if he sold to investors. The Canadian firm's offer came in under that, so even though they offered excellent resources, we decided not to partner with them. Besides, they could always submit an actual bid during a funding process, so it was more of a no-for-now than an outright rejection.

That left the status quo or a funding process. For this, we had to look at his situation. It seemed likely that, similar to what I had done, he could reject those offers and significantly increase his valuation by continuing along the same path for a few years. I didn't realize it at the time, but while the path I took did ultimately increase my valuation, it also posed a risk. If I had sold earlier, it would have given me a windfall that would have ensured my family's financial future right away. By continuing to grow, I kept the majority of my money and assets tied up in the business. If business had taken a sudden turn for the worse, or if something had happened to me, my family would have been in a precarious position.

Todd faced the same risk, but there was one big difference: age. When I got my first offers, I was in my early thirties. Todd was already in his forties. He had a family, and he was much closer to retirement age. If he went bankrupt, he'd have less time to make his money back and more obligations to handle. So I suggested he go through the process and sell part of his company. If he got $30 million, I told him to take $10 million off the table right away and save it, and take the other $20 million and grow the company as quickly as he could. He took my advice.

The point is that these decisions are deeply personal, and the best course of action usually depends on your goals and position in life.

Leverage Investor Expertise

The oldest investment firms have been around for over one hundred years. Any finance investor you might work with will likely have at least a decade of experience. All this knowledge, institutional and personal, adds up. These investors have helped scores of leaders grow successful companies. On top of all this knowledge they have a strong network and capital. All these resources can accelerate your growth, but only if you know how to leverage them. Companies that master leveraging their financing options can go from being moderately successful to an industry giant overnight.

Shortly after our second equity deal, my point of contact at Blackstone asked me what I wanted to do. I gave them an honest answer, that I want to own the oral wellness space. He responded, "That sounds great. Can we partner with you on it?"

In other words, they helped me become an investor by lending me some of their hard-earned business cachet. But this happened all because I took the time to develop a grand vision, and my level of conviction was high enough that I felt comfortable sharing it honestly with the people I worked with.

They also helped soothe Ideal Dental's growing pains. I have a standing meeting with my Blackstone team every Tuesday, right after my executive team meeting. In these meetings, I can bring any problem I'm struggling with to my support system, and they have the opportunity to recommend solutions. Usually they offer simple, effective fixes to problems that are novel to me but rote to them. For example, with the infusion of capital, we expanded at a much faster pace than ever before. Because of that, our cash flow suddenly became tight. We were opening almost as many offices as we had up and running, and even in the best circumstances it usually takes a month or two for a new office to turn a profit.

I mentioned to my Blackstone team that we might need to get creative to cover payroll until the new offices became profitable. They instantly asked me about our revolver, or standing line of credit with a bank. I told them what our revolver was, and the Blackstone people told me that in our new circumstances we needed a larger one. The next day we called the bank, and they agreed. They nearly doubled our revolver, and we used that money to cover expenses. It was a simple, even obvious, solution—the sort of solution that I or my CFO should have come up with. But we were flustered, we were growing. Blackstone had been there before, and they nudged us in the right direction. The key was that we communicated our struggles honestly and frequently with our support system.

EPILOGUE

From Good to Great to the Exit

Anyone can have one great day. They can get up early, get into the gym, drink a green smoothie for breakfast, and have a salad for lunch. They can go to work, or their business, and stay focused for ten hours, knocking everything they need to do out of the park. It's a great day.

But it doesn't make that person great.

Greatness isn't a one-time achievement. It's a journey, not a destination. It takes effort. Before you can even think about creating something great, you need to master good. And then you need to be good every day for at least ten to twenty years. All that effort will add up to something great.

It takes at least ten years of consistent hard work, dedication, perseverance, and resilience to begin building something great and leave a legacy.

But even that isn't enough. To create a truly enduring legacy, you need to maintain being great for decades. You need to find more commitment to the grind, get even better, and work smarter and harder. Then when you've dominated every day for decades, you'll have achieved the highest level imaginable. It takes at least ten years of consistent hard work, dedication, perseverance, and resilience to begin building something great and leave a legacy.

I always share that most things aren't over until we decide they are. This should be extremely motivational for every aspiring entrepreneur. Your dream ends when you give up; if you continue pursuing it, you will get there eventually. It may take longer and look different than what you had originally envisioned, but that is OK. There is no blueprint or secret sauce that fits all businesses because we are all different, and that is a thing of beauty. Be true to yourself and stick with your gut. Your vision will change and evolve as you grow as a person and business leader.

And in business, as in sports, there will be a time when it must end. The world changes. Customers change, technology changes, the challenges change. You will have been successful because you could tap into the zeitgeist of your time, your generation, and know what customers needed. Eventually you won't have that same knowledge. Your business can live on and still be great and innovate, but it will need the guidance of a new visionary. The truly great have the humility to know when their time has come. They bow out with grace and allow the next generation to carry the culture forward.

ACKNOWLEDGMENTS

My journey wouldn't be complete without the support of my wife, Julie. She has been alongside me from my days as a dental student dreaming up DECA to now witnessing what it has grown into. Thank you for always believing in me and supporting me through this bumpy journey. I love you.

To my four wonderful kids—Daniel, Sofia, Ella, and Rian. Each one of you is so special and unique. You have taught me the value of life and unconditional love. You have forced me to slow down and enjoy the moments that we can't put a value on. You have humbled me and made me more patient. I am a better person because of you.

To my parents—Riaz and Qaiser Ahmed. Thank you for all the sacrfices and giving me the opportunity to explore. Thank you for instilling and exemplifying the values of hard work, sacrifice, perseverance and true grit. Mom, I miss you every day. Your words and advice are reflected upon often, and when the pain is unbearable, I look up to the sky and find the brightest star and know you are looking over me from heaven.

To my DECA team (too many to mention). Thank you for your unwavering commitment and belief in me. We would not be here without the effort of each and every one of you. I feel like we are still in the trenches working endlessly to make this a better company for our patients (guests) and employees every single day.

To Shalin Patel, your boundless dedication, belief, and unwavering support over the last 15 years, from first associate dentist to friend, carry a very special place on this journey.

ENDNOTES

CHAPTER TWO

1. Chris Getman, “A Typical Plane Crash Involves 7 Consecutive Errors (So Does Your Failed Project),” Agency Arsenal, Nov. 30, 2018, https://theagencyarsenal.com/small-errors/#:~:text=A%20Typical%20Plane%20Crash%20Involves,So%20Does%20Your%20Failed%20Project).
2. Joanna Bailey, Jake Hardiman, and Riley Pickett, “How Flying Today Is Safer Than at Any Time in the Past,” Simple Flying, updated May 1, 2023, https://simpleflying.com/how-safe-is-flying/#:~:text=According%20to%20research%20by%20Harvard,are%20one%20in%2011%20million.
3. Kathy Kavan, “Feel like watching the Xerox demo that influenced Apple?” AnotherDesignBlog, October 19, 2012, https://kathykavan.posthaven.com/feel-like-watching-the-xerox-demo-that-influe.

CHAPTER THREE

1. Anthony Bourdain, “One Day—and One Night—in the Kitchen at Les Halles,” *The New Yorker*, April 9, 2000, https://www.newyorker.com/magazine/2021/09/06/magazine20000417hells-kitchen.

CHAPTER FOUR

1. Statista Research Department, "Advertising expenses of Uber Technologies from 2018 to 2022 (in billion U.S. dollars)," Statista, August 22, 2023, https://www.statista.com/statistics/1265542/uber-technologies-ad-spend/.
2. Elizabeth Segran, "These are the most hated brands in America at least according to Twitter," *Fast Company*, October 5, 2021, https://www.fastcompany.com/90682917/these-are-the-most-hated-brands-in-america.
3. Daniel Coyle, *The Culture Code: The Secrets of Highly Successful Groups* (New York: Bantam Books, 2018), 85.
4. Sian, "Mind Tricks Used Within the Food Industry," Smart Restaurants, April 3, 2017, http://www.smart-restaurants.co.uk/restaurants/mind-tricks-used-within-the-food-industry/; Steven T. Wright, "Why McDonald's Looks Sleek and Boring Now," Vox, November 1, 2021, https://www.vox.com/22736636/mcdonalds-design-aesthetic-look-buildings.
5. Charles Duhigg, "Is Amazon Unstoppable," *The New Yorker*, October 10, 2019, https://www.newyorker.com/magazine/2019/10/21/is-amazon-unstoppable.
6. Franck Louveau, "What Is Service Culture," EHL Insights, accessed October 4, 2023, https://hospitalityinsights.ehl.edu/service-culture-definition#:~:text=If%20you're%20looking%20for,to%20voluntarily%20quit%20the%20job.
7. Catherine Morin, "How the Ritz-Carlton Creates a 5 Star Customer Experience," CRM.org, December 13, 2019, https://crm.org/articles/ritz-carlton-gold-standards.

CHAPTER FIVE

1. Claire Cain Miller, et al, "Vast New Study Shows a Key to Reducing Poverty," *The New York Times*, August 1, 2022, https://www.nytimes.com/interactive/2022/08/01/upshot/rich-poor-friendships.html.

2. Jason Del Rey, "Leaked Amazon Memo Warns the Company Is Running Out of People to Hire," Vox, June 17, 2022, https://www.vox.com/recode/23170900/leaked-amazon-memo-warehouses-hiring-shortage.
3. Sophia Popova, "Chobani: Sour Milk Never Tasted So Sweet," Harvard Business School Digital Initiative, modified December 4, 2015, https://d3.harvard.edu/platform-rctom/submission/chobani-sour-milk-never-tasted-so-sweet/.

CHAPTER SEVEN

1. Danny Klein, "Dunkin' Brands CEO Nigel Travis Retires from Role," QSR, July 11, 2018, https://www.qsrmagazine.com/fast-food/dunkin-brands-ceo-nigel-travis-retires-role.
2. Sarah Hansen, "The Rise and Fall of General Electric (GE)," Investopedia, updated May 5, 2022, https://www.investopedia.com/insights/rise-and-fall-ge/.

CHAPTER EIGHT

1. Viktor Hendelmann, "Why Is Uber Not Profitable? Here Are 5 Reasons Affecting Its Bottom Line," Productmint, accessed October 11, 2023, https://productmint.com/why-is-uber-not-profitable/#:~:text=The%20delivery%20business%2C%20even%20with,basis%20back%20in%20Q3%202021.
2. Eliza Bavin, "Airbnb, Reddit, Deliveroo: Huge Companies that Have Never Made a Profit," Yahoo! Finance, April 18, 2022, https://au.finance.yahoo.com/news/companies-that-have-never-made-a-profit-011104731.html.
3. Jea Yu, "Is Uber Bait and Switching Its Way to Profitability," *Entrepreneur*, August 16, 2022, https://www.entrepreneur.com/finance/is-uber-bait-and-switching-its-way-to-profitability/433477#:~:text=Uber%20turned%20a%20profit%20on,in%20cash%20and%20cash%20equivalents.

4. Kellen Browning, "Uber Reports Record Revenue as It Defies the Economic Downturn," *The New York Times*, February 8, 2023, https://www.nytimes.com/2023/02/08/business/uber-revenue.html.
5. Ryan Vlastelica, "Tech Earnings Matter More Than Ever as the Bubble Deflates," Bloomberg, October 10, 2022, https://www.bloomberg.com/news/articles/2022-10-10/earnings-matter-more-than-ever-as-bubble-deflates-tech-watch?leadSource=uverify%20wall.
6. Noah Frank, "The Rise and Fall of Deadspin: How 'Jerks in Brooklyn' Changed Sports Journalism," *The Guardian*, July 21, 2022, https://www.theguardian.com/sport/2022/jul/21/the-rise-and-fall-of-deadspin-how-jerks-in-brooklyn-changed-sports-journalism; Ben Koo, "Deadspin's Traffic and Execution Will Both Need to Vastly Improve If the Site Wants to Survive in the Long Term," Awful Announcing, May 28, 2020, https://awfulannouncing.com/online-outlets/deadspin-traffic-execution-relaunch-great-hill-zombie.html.

ABOUT THE AUTHOR

Dr. Sulman Ahmed is the Founder, Chairman, and CEO of DECA Dental Group, the holding company for the consumer-facing brand Ideal Dental. He is the influential leader shaping and motivating DECA Dental's growth, strategy, and culture. In 2008, Dr. Ahmed opened his first dental office with a vow to establish a truly patient-centered model. Today, the rapidly growing brand represents approximately 200 locations in nine states, serving around 3,000 guests per day.

In his personal career, Dr. Ahmed has achieved many honors and awards, including receiving The University of Texas at Dallas Distinguished Alumni Award (2024). He has also been named the EY Entrepreneur of the Year (2017), one of Glassdoor's Top CEOs (2021) with a 98% approval rating, and one of *Dallas Business Journal*'s Most Admired CEOs (2023). He is also an in-demand speaker for national leadership, entrepreneurial, and motivational conferences.

Dr. Ahmed earned his Doctor of Dental Medicine degree from the Tufts University School of Dental Medicine and serves on their Board of Advisors. He is also President of the Association of Dental Support Organizations (ADSO), the premier association for businesses in the dental industry.

Connect with Dr. Sulman Ahmed on LinkedIn.